THE CHINESE ECONOMY

THE CHINESE ECONOMY

Structure and Reform in the Domestic Economy and in Foreign Trade

Wolfgang Klenner and **Kurt Wiesegart**

Transaction Books
New Brunswick (U.S.A.) and Oxford (U.K.)

Library of Congress Catalog Number: 84-16342
ISBN: 0-88738-612-1 (paper)
Printed in the United States of America

Library of Congress Cataloging in Publication Data

Klenner, Wolfgang.
  The Chinese economy.

  Bibliography: p.
  1. China—Economic policy—1976-   2. China—Commercial policy.
I. Wiesegart, Kurt.   II. Title.
HC427.92.K56 1984   338.951   84-16342
ISBN 0-88738-612-1 (pbk.)

P R E F A C E

This study deals with changes in the Chinese development strategy since the end of the Seventies. The new strategy also affects China's foreign trade. Accordingly, the present study not only analyzes the new internal development strategy, but also China's new foreign trade policy. The accomplished and planned changes in foreign trade aim at the expansion and diversification of foreign trade activities and at the enlargement of possibilities of utilizing foreign capital. Since reforms at various levels of Chinese foreign trade bodies are to create pre-conditions for the success of the new foreign trade policy, the institutional adjustment measures are broadly described, and an attempt is made to judge their potential effects.

The topic of this study is the result of expert talks between staff members of the Ministry of Economics of the Federal Republic of Germany and of the HWWA-Institute of Economic Research in Hamburg. The study which has been carried out under a contract with the Ministry of Economics was completed by the end of 1982. In order to make it available also to researchers as well as businessmen and officials in other countries, it is published in English.

Both authors have been dealing with the economic development of the PR China for ten years and have visited China several times for extended periods. While being in China for a five-months-period, by invitation of the Chinese Planning Commission, Dr. Klenner had intensive discussions on the subject of the study with members of the Planning Commission, the Economic Commission, the Foreign Trade Ministry, Chinese banks, and with various economic experts. Mr. Wiesegart, during his stay in China in 1982, analyzed problems of the Chinese raw material production and was particularly engaged in questions concerning the reform of the foreign trade systems.

Hamburg, May 1983

Klaus Bolz

C O N T E N T S

INDEX TO TABLES

INTRODUCTION

At the end of the seventies China's economic policymakers decided to broaden and intensify the country's foreign economic relations. They recognised that by participating more actively in the international division of labour, in other words by using contributions from abroad, they could modernise the country more smoothly and more quickly than would be possible if China relied on her own resources alone. China's trading partners are therefore faced with the problem of knowing the form in which China wishes to use foreign resources in future and in which sectors. This study attempts to answer that question by making a detailed analysis of Chinese development policy.

The opening of China's borders to trade from abroad is one element in a development policy that differs in several important respects from the previous concept. The fundamental development priorities have been modified and the guiding principle behind China's organisational policy has been revised. This change of direction has had a decisive influence on the country's external trade objectives, on the institutional structure of China's foreign trade system and hence on the foreign policy meas-ures pursued. If we are to be able to predict China's future foreign trade policy, we must subject her new development strategy to fairly wide-ranging examination.

The first part of the study therefore contains a detailed analysis of the change in the development concept at the end of the seventies. It examines the main characteristics of the previous development policy, the reasons for the change in orientation and the new aspects that have emerged. The measures taken since the change and the results achieved so far are then discribed. This serves as the basis for a number of interim conclusions about China's future external trade policy.

That policy is the focus of analysis in the next Chapter. A brief survey of external trade objectives is followed by a detailed examination of the most important measures taken to achieve them; these relate to the expansion and diversification of China's foreign trade activities and the employment of foreign capital. The modification of foreign trade institutions also belongs under this heading. The examination of institutional changes at central, regional and enterprise levels is designed to help China's western trading partners identify possible contacts and negotiators on the Chinese side. Finally, the most important findings of the study are presented in a short summary.

CHAPTER I

CHANGES IN DEVELOPMENT POLICY

1.   At the end of the seventies China's economic policymakers decided on a development strategy that differed in important respects from the policy followed previously. For example, expansion of the output of consumer goods and the raising of private incomes were to become the focus of development efforts and the extensive decentralisation of economic decision-making right down to the production unit was to provide scope for plant initiatives, although the central authorities would not be relinquishing control over the economy.[1]

The Chinese leadership brought about this change in development policy because certain economic problems with which they had been wrestling for some time could not be solved by means of the previous development plan; indeed , some of the problems were being caused by the plan itself. They also felt that their ambitious development goals could not be achieved under the previous policy.

The reasons for the change in development policy and the objective it served are examined more closely in the analysis that follows. First, however, the main characteristics of the previous development policy and their consequences shall be discussed.

1 The outline of the new economic concept was published in June 1979 at the   Second Session of the Fifth National People's Congress. Cf. Main Documents   of the Second Session of the Fifth National People's Congress of the People's Republic of China, Beijing 1979.

1. Characteristics of the previous development policy and its consequences

2.   The development concepts with which China's economic policy-makers experimented until the second half of the seventies show distinct differences in certain respects. For example, at the beginning of the fifties the government first attempted to get a grip on the economy by means of the strictest centralisation possible. At the end of the fifties, by contrast, the authorities wanted to involve the "masses" in the development process by delegating much of the power of decision to lower administrative levels[1] and to cast off the cloak of underdevelopment once and for all in a "great leap forward". There were too many failures, however, so that in the early sixties a programme of consolidation was begun which again gave the central authorities greater scope for decision-making. The Cultural Revolution, which began in the second half of the sixties, brought renewed shifts in power and changes in the direction of policy:[2] influence over economic decisions came to be exercised mainly by ideologically inspired party officials in the lower regional administrative units.[3]

3.   For all the differences, the concepts did have points in common, however. For example, in almost all the phases the proportion of national income devoted to capital formation was very high by international standards. For many years China's investment ratio was well over 30 per cent and in some periods even exceeded 40 per cent of the material national product.[4] (In China, as in the other centrally-planned economies, the national accounts are drawn up in accordance with the system of material product balances. The material national income is comparable

---

1 See, for example, ZHOU Zhuandian: Guanyu jiceng gongye qiye guanli zhidu de gaige wenti, in: Hongqi, No. 7, 1981, pp. 9 et seqq.

2 Cf. LI, Shucheng: Gaige qiye guanli jigou, cujin gongye shengchan de fazhan, in: Jingji Yanjiu, No. 4, 1965, p. 20.

3 With regard to the different planning and plant management concepts in the various development phases see KLENNER, Wolfgang: Ordnungs-prinzipien im Industrialisierungsprozeß der VR China, Hamburg 1979.

4 Cf. YANG Bo: Jilei he xiaofei guanxi de tantao, in: Hongqi, No. 6, pp. 13 et seqq.

14

with the net national product at factor cost less the value added of a few branches in the services sector, but is not identical with this aggregate.[1]) By way of comparison, India's investment ratio stood at 24 per cent in 1973.[2]

4. Investment was channelled mainly into heavy industry. As a rule, more than 50 per cent of state gross fixed capital formation went into the development of this sector.[3] It also had a prior call on other national resources, because economic progress was equated with industrialisation, which at that time was generally held to be determined by the level of heavy industrial production, particularly steel output.

5. In keeping with the policy of large-scale investment and the priority given to the development of heavy industry, incomes policy measures provided little scope for wage increases. The bulk of the growth in national income was used to expand the nation's capital stock and not to raise private incomes. The per capita incomes of the urban and rural population therefore showed only small rates of growth.

6. Another characteristic of the development concepts pursued hitherto was the very limited use of foreign resources to develop the economy. China feared that excessively close economic ties with other countries could place her in a position of dependence that would lay her open to economic and political blackmail and make it difficult for her to

1 With regard to the Chinese definition of national income see the essay by YUE Wei: Guomin shouru jusuan fangfa lun, in: Jingji Yanjiu, No. 3, 1956, pp. 48 et seqq. A more recent treatment of the Chinese national income concept is to be found in CHEN Zhibiao, Guomin shouru fanwei de chongxin kaocha, in: Jingji Yanjiu, No. 4, 1981, pp. 39 et seqq.

2 Cf. the examination of China's investment ratio compared with that of other countries in: KLENNER, Wolfgang, Der Wandel in der Entwicklungsstrategie der VR China. Umstrukturierung und Reform der chinesischen Wirtschaft seit 1978, Hamburg 1981, pp. 51 et seqq.

3 For example, between 1966 and 1978, 55.5 per cent of all state expenditure on capital construction went into heavy industry but only 5.15 per cent into light industry. Cf. LÜ Lüping, Guanyu jiasu fazhan qinggonggye de jige wenti, in: Jingji Yanjiu, No. 2, 1980, p. 30.

follow an independent development path. Hence for many years foreign trade was no more than a stop-gap. For the same reason the level of imports was determined by the amount of foreign currency earnings; the leadership also had strong reservations about external debt, not least for historical and ideological reasons.

7. It is less easy to recognise common features in the organisational policies pursued under the different development concepts, but they are there nonetheless. Although the division of economic powers among different administrative levels (central government, provinces, cities, districts and people's communes) was repeatedly re-organised, production units always remained bound by the directives of the economic administrators and had very little scope for taking their own decisions. A further constant was the fact that the prices at which enterprises purchased their intermediate inputs or sold their products were essentially set by the administration. In these circumstances decentralisation occurred only within the economic administration machine; there was practically no change in the degree to which production and trading enterprises were dependent on the relevant central ministries or local bureaux.

8. The previous development policy enabled China to achieve remarkable success in heavy industry, in other words in the area on which most of the development effort was concentrated. Between 1952 and 1980 the output of coal rose ninefold, the generation of electricity by a factor of 40, the production of raw materials by a factor of 27 and cement production by one of 26.[1] China is now well up among the leaders in the world league table for these commodities; she occupies third place in the world in the production of coal, primary energy and cement, fifth in raw steel output and ninth in the production of crude oil.

9. By contrast, production figures were unsatisfactory in the consumer goods sector, in which relatively little was being invested. In many

---

1 Cf. the production figures for 1952 in State Statistical Bureau: Ten Great Years; Peking 1960; and those for 1980 in Renmin Ribao, 30.4.1981.

years the increase in production was so low that with the rapid population growth[1] there was no notable improvement in the standard of living. For example, in 1978 the allocation of grain per head of the population was not much higher than in the mid fifties.[2] The supply of other food stuffs also remained very low; for instance, the annual per capita consumption of meat came to only 8.5 kg in 1979, as against 110-120 kg in the USA.[3] Edible oil and sugar were also in short supply; at the end of the seventies the annual consumption of sugar came to little more than 2 kg per head (as against 30 kg in Japan and 8 kg in India[4]) and even this low level could be reached only by importing considerable quantities. There were shortages of textiles, which were still rationed. In 1979 quotas of cotton cloth were little more than 5 metres per head (corresponding to less than 40 per cent of the world average) and were barely more generous than they had been in 1969.[5] Supplies of many consumer durables such as bicycles clocks, radios and furniture were also totally inadequate.[6]

10. The long-standing shortages in the consumer goods sector actually became a hindrance to development at the end of the seventies. The population had foregone consumer goods and made great development efforts for so many years that they finally wanted to share in the fruits of industrialisation and would accept no further postponement of consumer spending. This imposed distinct constraints on the previous development policy, with its emphasis on the highest possible investment in

1 The population rose from 550 million in 1949 to about 960 million in 1978.

2 Cf. WANG Meihan: Guanyu xiaofei jingjixue de jige lilun wenti, in: Jingji Yanjiu, No. 8, 1980, p. 38.

3 See The China Business Review, January-February 1980, p. 71.

4 Cf. Gongren Ribao, 15.4.1981.

5 Cf. WANG Meihan, loc. cit., p. 38.

6 Nevertheless China has become the world's largest producer of bicycles, sewing machines and cigarettes. In the production of wrist watches she is in fourth place in the world. See Xinhua News Agency News Bulletin (abbreviated to XNA hereafter), 2.7.1981.

heavy industry, so that the economic policymakers were forced to revise their thinking.

11. A further incentive to change lay in the lack of significant success in achieving continuous and balanced economic growth. Phases of economic progress were all to often followed by periods of serious setbacks. Admittedly, these setbacks can be attributed largely to natural causes in a country that is still as heavily dependent on agriculture as China, but battles over the direction of policy also had a prejudicial effect on the economy because of the close links between politics and economic activity in china. In the main, however, the reductions in growth rates were probably caused by the specific priorities of the old development strategy. [1]

It was not only the consumer goods sector that was in a bad way; other important sectors and branches were also neglected because the authorities had such a one-track interest in spectacular rates of growth in selected branches of heavy industry and consequently paid insufficient attention to links with other sectors and industries.[2] The result was economic imbalance, which repeatedly stunted growth in past decades. By 1978 the imbalance had become so serious that it was doubtful whether the previous development strategy had any sense at all.[3]

12. Growth in industry, which is still heavily dependent on agricultural inputs, was for example limited by the poor production figures for the neglected agricultural sector. The imbalance between sectors producing and raw materials on the one hand and manufacturing industry on the

1 See KLENNER, Wolfgang: Wirtschaftliche Entwicklung und strukturelle Ungleichgewichte in der Volksrepublik China, in: Osteuropa-Wirtschaft, No. 4, 1980, pp. 292 et seqq.

2 See WAN Quwu: Tiaozheng bili shixian shangpin gongxu pingheng, in: Jingji Yanjiu, No. 4, 1981, p. 17 et seqq.

3 See for example XU Dixin: Woguo dangqian jingji tiaozheng wenti, in: Jingji Yanjiu, No. 6, 1981, p. 3 et seqq.; GUI Shiyong, ZHOU Shu-lian: Lun jingji tiaozheng de mubiao, jieduan he cuoshi, in: Jingji Yanjiu, No. 6, 1982, p. 9 et seqq.

other also had a dampening effect. Shortages in the supply of fuels, energy and raw materials meant that even the manufacturing capacity that was available could not be fully utilised. There was also a shortage of transport capacity which impeded the division of labour between enterprises and between regions and hampered the realisation of specialisation advantages and productivity gains. In these circumstances a continuation of the previous policy would have been risky and might have foundered for lack of co-operation from the underpaid population.

13. The all-important organisational concepts also had to be viewed in a critical light. State enterprises had previously been bound by the directives of the economic authorities covering basically all matters except production itself, such as procurement, sales and investment in additional or replacement machinery. A smooth mode of operation had already proved very difficult in these circumstances, because all too often the economic administrators were ill-informed. Moreover, neither the economic authorities nor the enterprises were obliged by market mechanisms to match production to demand; as a consequence, many enterprises produced goods for which there was no demand, thus exacerbating the imbalances (paragraph 58).

As the economic interdependence among sectors grows in line with increasing development and specialisation, the retention of this organisational structure promised to magnify the problems that had already arisen. It was therefore realised that decentralisation of the economy right down to the level of the enterprise was urgently required if China was to enjoy steady growth.[1]

II. The re-orientation of development policy

14. In order to come to grips with the hitherto unsolved development problems, China's economic policymakers decided to change their development priorities and drew up a catalogue of procedural measures

1 Cf. XUE Muqiao: Zhongguo shehuizhuyi jingji wenti yanjiu, Beijing 1979, pp. 180 et seqq.

from which they expected quite specific development effects. These measures are to be accompanied by organisational reforms designed to give market forces an important role in the economic process and in this way create the conditions necessary for continuous, smooth and demand-oriented growth. The individual measures are described below.[1]

1)   New development priorities

15.   A larger share of national income than hitherto is to be made available for consumption by significantly reducing the investment ratio. Whereas at the end of the seventies investment still accounted for more than 36 per cent of the material national income, the proportion is to be cut to little more than one-quarter.[2]

The economic policymakers assume that with the present strong economic imbalance a substantial investment programme would only have limited growth effects in any case and that investments on the previous scale would simply lead to "overinvestment". Hence those projects that can be expected to have only a marginal effect on production have been shelved. Concentration on the most profitable investment plans would then create some room for wage increases without causing too great a slowdown in growth.

16.   The government believes that the trend rate of growth can even be accelerated by introducing quite specific additional measures which also form a central part of the new development concept.   Hence in spite

---

1   The principles of the new development strategy have been drawn from essays by leading economists in the prominent economic journals Jingji Yanjiu (Economic Research) or Jingji Guanli (Economic Management) and from political documents. Conversations with members of the State Planning Commission, the State Economic Commission and the Ministry of Foreign Trade were also helpful in portraying the new policy.

2   Cf. JIANG Junchen, ZHOU Chaoyang, SHEN Jun: Lun shengchan he shenghuo de guanxi wenti, in: Jingji Yanjiu, No. 9, 1980, pp. 53 et seqq.

of the reduction in the investment rates, it should be possible to reach a growth path that is steeper than that which could have been achieved if the development strategy had remained unchanged.

17. These measures include changes in the sectoral allocation of resources aimed at increasing the supply of consumer goods quickly and creating a sound infrastructure. Light industry and agriculture are to receive more investment funds than previously and are also to receive preference in the allocation of other resources. The transport sector, residential construction, the education system and the health system are also to be expanded more strongly than before in order to create the essential prerequisities for smooth long-term growth by establishing an infrastructure in the widest sense of the word. By contrast, there is to be a dramatic reduction in the funds provided for branches or heavy industry mainly or exclusively producing intermediate inputs of equipment for heavy industry itself, which had previously enjoyed priority. The development of the remaining branches of heavy industry, in which raw materials and equipment are produced for light industry, agriculture and for the development of the infrastructure, is to be strongly promoted.

The main aim of these measures is thus to provide fewer resources than before for branches producing intermediate inputs to meet heavy industry's own requirements and to make more resources available to other areas of the economy; however, in order to reduce the investment ratio, the investment cuts for the first group of industries are to exceed by as much as possible the increases in investment in all other branches together.

18. Once a production structure has been created that brings a marked improvement in the supply of consumer goods and public-sector goods and services, it may again become necessary to channel more resources into branches producing for heavy industry's "own requirements". In those circumstances the investment ratio may have to be increased once again, but it should never return to its earlier high level. Whatever happens, demand will be the ultimate determining factor for all invest-

ment. Increases in production for their own sake - as previously happened in heavy industry - should not recur.

19. The changes in sectoral priorities are expected to have quite specific effects on growth. It is hoped that investment in light industry, where plant can be built and brought into production in a fairly short space of time, will produce high growth rates quickly.[1] It is assumed that investment in the branches of heavy industry producing plant or intermediate inputs for light industry or agriculture will also lead to relatively rapid growth but not so soon. By contrast, it is only in the long term that growth effects derive from investment in the energy sector (where projects usually take a long time to reach completion) and in infrastructure, but the development of these sectors is considered an important requirement for the increasing division of labour and hence for high rates of growth over the long term.

20. The opening of the country's borders to foreign trade is also a facet of the new development concept. Foreign plant and machinery are to be employed to promote restructuring and an acceleration in growth. Imports of capital goods are expected to bring particularly great advantages, as they will increase the proportion of production facilities with higher productivity rates (in comparison with plants manufactured in China). They are also expected to produce benefits by helping to remove bottlenecks in the Chinese economy and by teaching the population about technology, so that over the longer term they will also contribute towards raising the productivity of home-produced plant.

21. Although in principle productivity can be increased more quickly by importing modern plant than by producing plant in China, the government is aware that the scale of growth effects is not necessarily proportional to the volume of foreign equipment imported. It depends

---

1 Projects in light industry have usually been amortised in one year and ten months on average, whereas it takes five years and seven months in heavy industry. Cf. LI Long: Guanche tiaozheng fangzhen da li fazhan xiaofeipin shengchan, in: Jingji Yanjiu, No. 5, 1981, p. 6.

much more on having the right combination of foreign and domestic capital goods, in other words on ensuring that in importing foreign technology the limits to the absorption fo foreign capital are not exceeded.

22. A further measure consists in substantial increases in the incomes of the urban and rural population. In fact, two separate but superimposed incomes policy measures are involved here. As the economic policymakers hold the view that the consumption sacrifice was "too high" in past years, incomes are to be raised across the board by more that the current rate of productivity increase - as compensation, as it were, for income not received in the past. (Such general and unconditional wage increases for broad sections of the population require a reduction in the investment ratio if one ignores the possibility of substituting foreign capital for domestic saving on a larger scale, a possibility that is not considered by China.) On top of this there are to be individual increases in income in the form of bonuses linked to increases in output.

23. As wage increases across the board will quell or at least subdue the discontent that paralyses the economy, it ist expected that the population will identify itself with the economic programme. The linking of output and income will permit increases in individual incomes commensurate with greater effort, so that it is hoped that the motivation to work will also be increased. It is assumed that plant resources will be used more efficiently as a result, which should lead to productivity gains and, as with the changes in the investment structure and the introduction of foreign plant and equipment, to an acceleration in economic growth.

2)   The new organisational configuration

24. The procedural measures are to be accompanied by a number of reforms of organisational policy aimed at modifying the relationship between central and regional administrations and, above all, giving

enterprises greater independence.[1] It is intended that they should be less strictly bound by directives from the authorities and more receptive to market forces, which should induce them to match production to demand. The procurement of capital and other factors of production, the matching of production to demand and the sale of their products are to be largely their independent responsibility. In this way plant are to be given the opportunity to make their own contribution towards removing economic imbalances; indeed, they will be forced to do so by economic mechanisms, or less as a counterweight to state planning.

25. Nevertheless, the introduction of market forces on at least a temporary basis is not intended to produce a switch to a "market economy" in which the means of production are owned by the state. The government wants to exploit the dynamism, flexibility and initiative of individual firms, but the reins of the economy are to remain in the hands of the state. The government will continue to control the production and allocation of important goods (paragraphs 26-28), keep a check on investment (paragraph 29), monitor prices (paragraphs 30-31) and determine the framework for income distribution (paragraph 32), while allowing some scope for action by individual businesses.[2]

26. The state intends to continue to determine the level of production and the allocation of selected goods considered to be economically important so that state projects, regions, sectors of the economy or population groups are supplied with the necessary goods and factors of production. As a matter of principle, enterprises producing the goods in

1 Reforms are also taking place in agriculture. In this study the emphasis has been placed on reforms in the industrial sphere.

2 See for example XUE Muqiao: Zhongguo shehuizhuyi ..., loc. cit.; YANG Jisheng: Lilun lantu shiyan tiaojian, in: Jingji Yanjiu, No. 4, 1982, pp. 18 et seqq.; WU Zhenkun: Guanyu jianchi jihua jingji wei zhu, shichang tiaojie wei fu de jige wenti, in: Wuzi Guanli, No. 5, 1982, pp. 7 et seqq. YOU Lin: Gaijin jingji tizhi de zhongyao zhidao wenjian, in: Hongqi, No. 2, 1982, pp. 31 et seqq.; HUANG Zhenqi: Dui guoying qiye kuoda jingying quanli zizhuquan jige wenti de taolun, in: Jingji Yanjiu, No. 3, 1982, pp. 39 et seqq.; other sources: notes by KLENNER, Wolfgang on his conversations with members of the Economic Commission and the Planning Commission.

question will continue to be managed directly by the state administration.

It has not yet been decided precisely which products and enterprises fall into this category. It would appear to comprise some hundred products such as coal, building timber, a few kinds of steel and certain basic chemicals. These products are mainly produced in large modern plant which account for a very small proportion of the total numer of enterprises (300 000-400 000), but according to estimates by the Planning Commission, control over such plant enables the state to keep a hold on 20-30 per cent of the gross value of industrial production.

27.   In the case of goods that are also of great economic importance but available in sufficiently large quantities, the state does not wish to intervene directly in production (by setting quantities) or in distribution. (It is not yet clear which of the goods previously distributed centrally are involved here.) Enterprises that produce such goods will have considerable freedom of decision, but the state will draw up production and allocation guidelines and use appropriate economic instruments to enforce them. What the authorities have in mind is a system of economic levers (price policy, interest rate policy or fiscal policy) whereby the profitability of enterprises will be influenced in such a way that considerations of profit will themselves induce firms to take production and investment decisions consistent with state objectives.

28.   No direct management and control over other goods is envisaged; at most, guidance will be indirect and at arm's length. These are mainly goods such as might be sold in supermarkets: stationery, toys, textiles made of artificial fibres, shoes or crockery. They run to several hundred thousand items and although they are very important to the population, they have no significance for the development strategy nor are they essentials. According to Chinese sources they account for perhaps 20-30 per cent of the gross value of industrial production.

29.   In order to maintain control over the volume of investment and its sectoral and regional composition the state intends to continue to provide

a fairly substantial part of the capital for new projects from the budget. However, enterprises will for the first time be able to retain part of their profits as working funds and to use them for investment. Banks will also be able to lend to enterprises in accordance with their ability to repay the funds, in other words on the basis of profitability. (Up to now banks had mainly provided capital on an interest-free irredeemable basis for invest projects lauched by the economic authorities. Investment financed from enterprises' own funds and from borrowing will still be subject to some state control and guidance, such as the authorisation requirement for projects that exceed a certain value, interest rate differentials according to branch and region, etc.)[1]

30. The prices of goods that are of particular economic importance such as foodstuffs are to remain under state control, but apart from this the previous system of administered prices is to be eased. Price controls on a large proportion of goods are to be removed in stages; for example, upper or lower price limits will first be set in order to prevent excessive fluctuations. In this way a structure of scarcity prices may gradually evolve.

31. In addition, the following approach to price setting is under discussion with regard to certain products such as coal or steel. The government wants to bring prices gradually into line with unit costs, as the production conditions for some products have changed fundamentally since the freezing of many prices at the beginning of the fifties - for example, the production costs of many manufactured goods have fallen because of the introduction of mass production whereas the prices for certain mining products have risen because increasingly difficult deposits have been exploited. In these cases prices are to equal the average unit costs of the branch plus a profit margin (e.g. a set proportion of the capital employed). Prices set in this way would not, however, be scarcity prices.

1 Cf. XUE Muqiao: Jingji guanli tizhi gaige wenti, in: Hongqi, No. 8, 1979, p. 19.

32. Finally, the state intends to continue to determine the framework for income distribution. Wage rates for workers and employees will be set by the state in accordance with uniform criteria, but here too an easing of constraints is envisaged. Enterprises will be able to use their working funds financed from profits not only for investment purposes but also to pay performance bonuses to their staff and to offset part of any operating losses. Performance-linked bonuses and deductions, which will be limited in amount by state regulation, will thus to some extend alter the state wages structure to reflect the performance of plant and individuals.

As in the past, the state intends to influence the incomes of the rural population mainly by setting the purchasing prices of important food-stuffs and the selling prices of essential industrial inputs. Subsidies will be paid in the event of crop failures. Apart from this, farmers are to have considerable freedom of decision over their activities and there-fore be responsible for their own incomes.[1]

III. Implementation of the new development policy

33. Three years have now passed since approval was given to the new development strategy comprising the procedural and organisational measures described above. The question arises what has been done so far and what has been achieved. The following section attempts to answer that question in the light of the information available from Chinese sources. The first part of the analysis deals with procedural policy and examines the various measures taken to reduce the invest-ment ratio, modify production structures, exploit foreign capital goods and increase private incomes.

---

1 Cf. ZHAN Wu, LIU Wenpu: San zhong quanhui kaichuang le woguo nongye fazhan de xin luzi, in: Hongqi, No. 17, 1982, pp. 17 et seqq.

1) Procedural measures

A Reduction of the investment ratio

34. In order to lower the investment ratio the state took steps to reduce capital formation in the state and co-operative sectors. The state sector comprises primarily state enterprises (production units, transport companies or trading companies) that are run by the central government or by regional administrative units (provinces, cities, districts, counties). The co-operative sector consists mainly of agricultural producers' co-operatives and the small industrial and transport enterprises that they have set up and run.

At present well over half of all investment is undertaken by the central government, the regional administrations or state enterprises themselves. The central government and regional administrations finance their investment from taxes, profits transferred to them from enterprises and in certain circumstances bank loans. Investment carried out independently by state enterprises is financed from retained profits or, now that banks lend to enterprises, from bank loans.

The bulk of investment in the co-operative sector comes from the co-operatives themselves. They earn the necessary funds through their agricultural activities or from their industrial and transport enterprises. In addition to this there is investment by means of so-called "direct work accumulation", such as work on the construction of roads, dykes, dams or houses. The state does not normally finance co-operative investment except in the case of selected projects such as major irrigation schemes.

35. Before the reforms at the end of the seventies the central government had wide-ranging powers to determine and control the volume of investment in the economy, the composition of investment and even individual investment projects in both the state and co-operative sectors. The central government not only had responsibility for the bulk of investment undertaken by itself, but it also exercised tight control

over investment by regional authorities and state enterprises (whose share of overall investment was small), as these were strictly bound by the government's directives. It also had sufficient means of intervention to achieve its wishes with regard to the volume and composition of investment in the co-operative sector too: as the prices of the most important agricultural products and industrial inputs are set by the state, the latter could significantly influence the turnover and costs of agricultural enterprises and hence the level of their profits, which largely determined their ability to finance investment. The state also frequently exercised a direct influence on the investment decisions of co-operatives because the senior officials of producers' co-operatives were obliged to implement the development guidelines of the party or higher administrative units.

The reforms reduced the central government's ability to influence investment decisions in both the state and co-operative sectors. (The powers of decision over investment projects were delegated to lower regional administrations, enterprises and banks in order to stimulate initiative and a sense of responsibility and thus achieve better investment overall.) The central government's share in state investment therefore fell, but that of regional administrations and state enterprise rose. The central government's influence on the investment decisions of these bodies also weakened. Furthermore, banks no longer finance investments solely on instructions from the Ministry of Finance but could grant loans to enterprises on their own initiative on the basis of economic criteria (paragraph 107).

Changes also ocurred in the co-operative sector. As a result of far-reaching reforms in the system of rural collectives, agricultural households replaced production teams as the most important decision-makers in the production field; households were more strongly motivated towards maximising incomes and less towards achieving plan targets. This change greatly weakened the position of the senior co-operative officials, who had previously played a decisive role in enforcing central government guidelines in the co-operatives.

36. The question arises, how China's economic policymakers could achieve their objective of reducing the investment ratio in these changed organisational circumstances. To answer that question would require an examination of changes in the individual components of investment; however, no comprehensive statistics are available at present. A few isolated figures can be gleaned from state budget publications, but these throw little light on investment in the state sector as investments are now being financed increasingly by borrowing or self-financing rather than through grants. (The data collection system is still largely tailored to suit the previous organisational concept, so that even the Chinese authorities sometimes have difficulty gaining a detailed picture of investment.)

At present, however, the state budget ist still one of the prime sources of information on investment, first because the grant system still accounts for a substantial amount of investment and secondly because in principle, at least, the banks must operate within the loan funds allocated to them in the budget. Distinctions are made between the following components of investment: capital construction investment[1] (broadly comparable with gross fixed capital formation under the western system of statistical classification but noch quite identical), investment to increase current assets (stocks of goods with a life of less than one year and a value of 500 Yuan or less.);[2] investment to increase state reserves (these comprise chiefly the state's emergency grain reserves) and investment to "fully realise the potential of existing plant, for technical conversion and for production trials"[3] (this chiefly comprises investment to generate intensive growth, such as the re-equipping and

1 Cf. YUE Wei: Guomin shouru jisuan fangfa lun, in: Jingjiu Yanjiu No. 3, 1956, pp. 48 et seqq.; PENG Rongquan: Di wu jiang: Jiben jianshe jihua biaoge, in: Jihua Jingji, No. 5 1957, pp. 29 et seqq.; or ISHIKAWA, Shigeru: National Income and Capital Formation in Mainland China - An Examination of Official Statistics, Tokyo 1965, pp. 5 et seqq.

2 Cf. YAN Cuiyou: Tigao guding zichan biaozhun bu shi guangda qiye quanxian de zhengque zuofa, in: Jihua Jingji, No. 6, 1957, p. 23.

3 Cf. XNA, 30.6.1979; XNA, 16.4.1981.

modernisation of existing plant, the conversion of production programmes, etc.). In spite of the inadequacy of statistics on individual investment components, an attempt will be made to paint a rough picture of investment activity.

37. The largest and economically most important investment component is state capital construction investment, which came to 47.9 billion Yuan in 1978.[1] (1978 will be used here as base year and for purposes of comparison, because on the whole the "old" development strategy was followed until 1978.) In 1979, the first year in which the new development strategy was to be used, it rose to about 50 billion Yuan,[2] and a year later it even increased to 53.9 billion Yuan.[3] That represented an annual rate of growth of about 4 per cent in 1979 and about 8 per cent in 1980. As national income grew by about 7 per cent in each of these years,[4] the state's capital construction policy did little or nothing to help reduce the investment ratio in the years up to 1980.

38. Before 1980 the growth rates of the other investment components were curtailed somewhat. Investment in current assets and investment designed to harness plant potential, as it is called in Chinese terminology, were increased little, if at all.

The state exerted considerable pressure on rural co-operatives to postpone their construction projects. There were even instances in which uneconomic co-operative plant were closed down because they were competing with state enterprises for particularly scarce materials.

---

1 Cf. Communiqué of the State Statistical Bureau of the People's Republic of China on Fulfilment of China's 1978 National Economic Plan (27th June 1979), pp. 32 et seqq., (referred to subsequently as Communiqué 1978).

2 Cf. Communiqué of the State Statistical Bureau of the People's Republic of China on Fulfilment of China's 1979 National Economic Plan (30th April 1980) (referred to subsequently as Communiqué 1979).

3 Cf. Renmin Ribao, 30.4.1980.

4 Cf. Communiqués 1978 and 1979; Renmin Ribao, 30.4.1980.

39. The investment policy caused the investment ratio to decline by about 3 percentage points to 33.6 per cent in 1979 and to diminish further to 31 per cent in 1980.[1] Hence after two years in which a reduction in the investment ratio had been party policy in China was still far from her objective of cutting the ratio to about one-quarter of national income. As stated above, the authorities had planned to raise the marginal productivity of capital by concentrating on a few viable investment projects so that relatively high growth rates would be achieved even with a low investment ratio. The behaviour of the ratio indicates that the intended rigorous selection of investment projects was not in operation by 1980, at least in the state sector (for the reasons, see paragraph 61).

40. In order finally to make greater progress with reducing the investment ratio, a drastic cut in state capital construction investment was decided at the beginning of 1981 - instead of 55 billion Yuan as originally planned, only 30 billion Yuan would initially be spent on capital construction.[2] However, this radical cut, which had been decided after the beginning of the fiscal year, was soon revised upwards to 38 billion Yuan. In the event, expenditure on capital construction projects came to 42.8 billion Yuan,[3] but this was still about 11 billion Yuan less than in 1980.

There was an increase in investment to harness plant potential, in other words investment in modernisation, which was largely financed by the banks. Care was taken, however, not to outweigh the reduction in capital construction investment, so that in 1981 the investment ratio fell to just under 30 per cent.[4]

---

1 With regard to the gradual realisation of the new development strategy see GUI Shiyong, ZHOU Shulian: Lun jingji tiaozheng de mubiao, jieduan he cuoshi, in: Jingji Yanjiu, No. 6, 1981, pp. 9 et seqq. See also YANG Bo: Jilei he xiaofei guanxi de tantao, in: Hongqi, No. 6, 1981, p. 14.

2 Cf. XNA, 31.8.1980, and LIU Lixin, TIAN Chunsheng: Zenyang renshi yasuo jiben jianshe guimo, in: Hongqi, No. 8, 1981, p. 9.

3 Cf. Communiqué of the State Statistical Bureau of the People's Republic of China on Fulfilment of China's 1981 National Economic Plan (29th April 1982) (referred to subsequently as Communiqué 1981).

4 Cf. XU Dixin: Woguo dangqian jingji tiaozheng wenti, in: Jingji Yanjiu, No. 6, 1981, p. 4.

41. In the 1982 budget plan state capital construction investment was set at 38 billion Yuan, about 5 billion Yuan less than in 1981. Of this amount, 29.7 billion Yuan is to be disbursed through the budget[1] and the rest is to be financed by enterprises themselves or by the banks. As a considerable part of the funds are earmarked for the completion of projects in hand, the cuts in capital construction investment mean that not too many new projects are to be begun and those will be in sectors that have been given the highest priority (light industry, energy, infrastructure).

42. The 1982 economic plan provided for investment totalling 25 billion Yuan to harness plant potential, in other words for modernisation; 5 billion Yuan is to come from the budget and the rest is to be financed by enterprises themselves or through bank loans.[2] All sources agree that this amount far exceeds the estimates for previous years. It is not apparent from published plan data how far the estimates of other investment components were influenced by the aim of reducing the investment ratio. Plan figures for various budget items are available, but they do not give a sufficiently accurate picture, as enterprises have been given considerably greater freedom to finance themselves and to raise loans. In view of the substantial sums set aside for modernisation investment, there is unlikely to be any dramatic reduction in the investment ratio in 1982.

43. Chinese exports have long argued for a significant increase in that part of investment that serves not to create new production capacity but to modernise existing plant, in other words to intensify economic growth.[3] For example, Sun Yefang, one of China's most competent economists, has demanded that more than half of all investment be devoted to promoting intensive growth. The composition of investment in the 1982 economic plan shows that China's economic policymakers are now

---

1 Cf. Renmin Ribao, 6.5.1982.

2 Cf. Renmin Ribao, 6.5.1982.

3 Cf. See for example, Zai tiaozheng zhong zouchu yi tiao fazhan jing-ji de xin luzi, in: Hongqi, No. 7, 1981, pp. 6 et seqq.

serious about the modernisation of existing plant and are providing large sums for this purpose.

The authorities plan to begin replacing machinery in only a small number of factories at first. The capital required to modernise China's plant is estimated to be so high that they do not feel able to proceed on a broad front. In the next few years an even lager volume of funds is to be used for this purpose. The view is now being expressed that the economy could absorb more investment oriented towards modernisation than had been assumed in 1978. If this interpretation gains acceptance, the desirable investment ratio would probably work out somewhat higher than originally planned (25 per cent).

44. The new policy orientation could lead to more than just the imports of technology to be financed by China herself; as the capital require- ment for modernisation is extremely large and as it has already been decided to raise incomes, larger quantities of capital than originally intended might possibly be imported, either in loans or in other forms of capital procurement such as joint ventures, compensatory trade deals and the like.

45. Other interesting possibilities are also emerging. At present the State Economic Commission and other bodies are deliberating which enterprises or sectors should be modernised first. For the moment the central authorities will continue to set the direction of the modernisation process, but there are plans for a considerable degree of decentralisa- tion over the medium term. Individual enterprises are to discover their own weakenesses and to invest accordingly. It might then prove advan- tageous to give enterprises themselves the opportunity to investigate whether the world market can offer appropriate solutions to their prob- lems. The admittedly limited devolution of foreign trade decisions right down to enterprise level - which also presupposes the availability of foreign currency - does not necessarily rule out the co-ordination and supervision of import decisions by competent bodies. It would therefore seem appropriate for China's trading partners to ascertain the modern- isation requirements of Chinese firms on the spot and to offer them suitable technical solutions or equipment.

34

B   Modification of the structure of production

46. Adaptation of the production structures to the new development priorities ocurred essentially on two levels. First, it involved the re-organisation of relations among the sectors. i.e. the global relations between heavy industry, light industry and infrastructure in the broad sense, and secondly it concerned the rearrangement of relations among the individual branches within the sectors and the fine tuning of plant production programmes.

a)   Restructuring of relations among the most important sectors

47. Let us first examine the initial steps towards reorganisation of sectoral relationships since 1978. They consist essentially in changes in the sectoral composition of investment, policy adjustments in the allo-cation of resources other than capital and the conversion of production in existing plant.

The rates of growth in the gross production values for the various sector will be used to assess the success of the measures taken (para-graph 57). Gross production values are not particularly suitable, for they cover all inputs at every stage of production and give no indica-tion whether the goods produced found a market (a particularly acute problem in China, where unwanted goods to the value of billions of Yuan have been produced that satisfy the economy's needs in no way whatever and yet inflate the statistical value of production). However, in view of the limited statistical material available, there are no better indicators.

48. Data on the sectoral composition of investment are available prima-rily for capital construction investment financed through the budget, although not for all years of the period of interest here. It is difficult to obtain an accurate picture of sectoral investment solely on the basis of the distribution of capital construction investment financed through the budget because the proportion of investment financed in other ways

is increasing as a result of the economic reforms. (Reports on the state budget occasionally also include information on extra-budgetary investment.) Additional details may sometimes be gleaned from the economic plans, but not with regard to the co-operative sector, where the necessary capital is raised by co-operative members themselves and does not appear in the state plan at all. (Overall investment in agriculture, for instance, is therefore much higher than the amount financed by the state.) Sectoral shares in state capital construction investment must therefore be treated with due caution if they are to be used to assess the composition of investment in the economy.

In 1979 the state budget reflected at least the general trend of the new development priorities, with its provision for an increase in investment in agriculture as a proportion of total state capital construction investment from 10.7 per cent in 1978 to 14 per cent. The share for light industry was also to be raised, although only from 5.4 per cent in 1978 to 5.8 per cent in 1979. By contrast, the planned share for heavy industry was trimmed from 55 per cent in 1978 to only 46.8 per cent in 1979.[1]

These were only the plan data, however; as the 1979 budget estimates were greatly exceeded, it is to be assumed that the sectoral investment shares were not changed as intended. Precise data are available on state capital construction investment in light industry; the figure of 6.4 per cent of effective state capital construction investment[2] was higher than planned. According to all the information available, investment in heavy industry was also higher than planned, both in absolute terms and as a percentage of the total.

From 1978 to 1979 there was an extraordinarily high rate of growth in investment in the "non-productive" sector such as housing construction, the health service, the education system of research. This sector re-

1   Cf. ZHANG Jingfu: Report on the Final State Accounts for 1978 and
    the Draft State Budget for 1979, in: Main Documents of the Second
    Session of the Fifth National People's Congress of the People's
    Republic of China, Peking, 1979, p. 166.

2   Cf. XNA, 30.4.1981.

ceived more than one-quarter (13.5 billion Yuan) of all effective state capital construction investment,[1] 5.5 billion Yuan more than in 1978.

49. In 1980 the second year of the restructuring phase, a further shift in state capital construction investment occurred in favour of those branches of activity that were to receive priority under the new development strategy. Light industry's share of such investment (53.9 billion Yuan) rose to 9.1 per cent and that of the "non-productive" sector to 33.6 per cent. The largest expenditure within the latter was allocated to residential construction in order to improve the disastrous urban housing situation; as a proportion of total state capital construction investment, residential construction thus rose from 14.8 per cent in 1979 to 20 per cent in 1980.[2]

50. As mentioned above (paragraph 40), drastic cuts were made in the investment budget in 1981. Heavy industry was most strongly affected. Many planned building schemes were shelved and a few projects that had begun were even halted. On the other hand, the volume of investment for the development of light industry was not to be less than in 1980. According to the report on the final state accounts for 1981, 4.3 billion Yuan, or about 10 per cent of total state capital construction investment, was allocated to capital construction projects in light industry. Gross fixed capital formation in the non-productive sector came to 17.6 billion Yuan, 41 per cent of state capital construction investment, with residential construction accounting for 20.5 per cent.

51. Under the development plans drawn up at the end of the seventies the state was to inject large sums into agriculture; it was envisaged that agriculture's share of state capital construction investment would be increased to 18 per cent by 1985.[3] Agricultural investment seems hardly to have risen so far, so that the sector seems to have been left to rely on its own resources again, buth with one difference: previously it had been thought that the best conditions for a rapid expan-

1 Cf. Communiqué 1979, p. 39.
2 Cf. Ta Kung Pao, 25.6.1981.
3 Cf. Beijing Rundschau, No. 12, 1980, p. 17.

sion of agricultural production could be created by strengthening the collective and gradually increasing the size of collective production units; now energies are to be mobilised by devolving power right down to the individual households.

52. In the years from 1978 to 1981 the most conspicuous changes were the rise in the non-productive sector's share in state investment from just over 17 per cent to over 40 per cent and the sharp increase in light industry's share from little over 5 per cent to 10 per cent. It should be noted, however, that since the investment cuts in 1981 relative share do indicate something about development priorities but not much about the trend of the absolute figures; moreover, it should be recalled once again that the significance of the figures is also reduced by the fact that the economic reforms have increasingly permitted production units access to additional sources of investment that are not necessarily reflected in the available statistics. (The estimated sectoral composition of total gross fixed investment for 1977-79 contained in the World Bank Report on China may be taken by way of example; this puts the respective shares at 21 per cent for agriculture, 47 per cent for heavy industry, 10 per cent for light industry and 23 per cent for other sectors.)

53. Implementation of the new development priorities also entailed giving preference to agriculture and projects in the non-productive sector in the supply of raw materials, energy and transport. Energy was particularly important in this connection; it is in such short supply that in 1978 only 70-80 per cent of industrial production capacity could be utilised for lack of energy (paragraph 67). As energy production cannot be increased in the short term, the supply to individual factories or branches of industry can be improved only at the expense of others. Hence, more energy can be provided to agriculture and light industry only if heavy industry, which consumes by far the largest share of the energy produced, receives correspondingly less. (Nevertheless, if effective short-term conservation measures were taken, energy reductions would not necessarily lead to proportionate cuts in production.)

54. It is difficult to quantify the extent to which the above allocation targets have been achieved. The supply of scarce factors of production to sectors that were to be given priority seems to have shown at least a trend improvement. The authorities were often ready to give preference in the provision of energy and other production factors to sectors on which development efforts were concentrated, even if this was at the expense of heavy industry and the capacity utilisation rate there declined further.

Studies had shown that the generation of a gross production value of 100 Yuan required more than three times as much electricity and almost five times as much coal in heavy industry as in light industry. Expressed another way, for the consumption of a given quantity of electricity light industry can produce more than three times as much as heavy industry in terms of value. This means that by cutting production by 100 Yuan in heavy industry enough electricity can be saved to produce goods worth more than 300 Yuan in light industry.[1]

Textile manufacturers and other light industrial firms that found themselves able to exploit their capacity to the full thanks to the better supply of energy often had a correspondingly higher requirement for working capital. So that a capital shortage should not lead to bottlenecks in these cases, the banks were instructed to give such enterprises priority in the provision of funds. According to the information available, the banking system seems to have followed the wishes of the economic policymakers and thus to have promoted the process restructuring.[2]

55. Realisation of the new development priorities also involved making appropriate changes in the production programmes of existing plant. Certain state-run enterprises in heavy industry (mainly modern plant forming part of the military equipment industry) were directed to include light industrial products such as bicycles or electric fans in their production programmes.

1 Cf. SONG Liwen: Lun da li zengjia xiaofeipin shengchan, in: Hong-qi, No. 6, 1981, p. 8.
2 Cf. Ta Kung Pao, 25.6.1981.

56. Switches in production also stemmed from the factory reforms. As selected plant were given wider powers of decision and could gear their production programme at least partly towards profit, factories in heavy industry also became interested in producing consumer goods, as these generally earned higher profits than heavy industrial products. Similar effects were also apparent in agriculture. Once the state's relatively strict crop planning machinery had been relaxed, the agricultural co-operatives took advantage of local conditions to produce greater quantities of commodities that command high prices.[1]

57. Taken together, these measures helped produce a change in the gross production values of the various sectors of the economy that broadly reflected the new development priorities. In 1979 the gross production value of agriculture rose by 8.6 per cent and that of industry increased by 8.5 per cent in relation to 1978. The rate of growth in agriculture thus exceeded that of industry. Light industry grew by 9.6 per cent, outperforming heavy industry, which recorded a rate of 7.7 per cent. This was still not sufficient, however, to bring about an appreciable change in the underlying sectoral structure of the economy.[2]

It was not until 1980 that the measures taken under the new economic programme began to bite. The gross production value of light industry recorded an exceptionally high rate of increase of 18.4 per cent, whereas that of heavy industry rose by only 1.4 per cent. The ratio between light and heavy industry therefore shifted markedly in favour of the former. There were problems in agriculture, however. It was shown once again that at the sector's present stage of development output does not depend solely on the factors employed. Natural disasters in the provinces of Hebei and Hubei caused serious regional crop shortfalls and famine that affected more than 20 million people. For this reason agricultural production rose by only 2.7 per cent, far less than in the

1 Cf. Gongren Ribao, 15.4.1981 and 16.4.1981.
2 Cf. Communiqué 1979, pp. 29 et seqq.

previous year.[1] However, in the light of the serious crop failures this is still a remarkable achievement that may be attributed primarily to the success of the economic reforms, which are increasingly enabling agricultural producers' co-operatives and, above all, individual households to produce for the highest possible profit.

In 1981 the rate of growth in agricultural production was again relatively high, 5.7 per cent. The gross production value of industry rose by 4.1 per cent; light industry again recorded a very high growth rate of 14.1 per cent while heavy industry showed a contraction of 4.7 per cent.[2] This decline indicates that the high growth rate in light industry was achieved mainly by diverting factors of production from heavy industry to light industry and that the capacity utilisation rate in the former declined further.

For 1982 growth rates of 4 per cent in the gross value of both agricultural and industrial production are planned, with light industry showing a rise of 7 per cent and heavy industry one of 1 per cent.[3] Light industry should thus continue to grow more rapidly than heavy industry, so that light industry's share of the gross value of industrial production will increase further, having already risen from 42.7 per cent to 51.4 per cent between 1978 and 1981.[4]

1 Cf. Renmin Ribao, 30.4.1981.

2 Cf. Communiqué 1981.

3 Cf. Renmin Ribao, 6.5.1982.

4 Cf. See for example SHAO Ying: An shehuizhuyi jiben jingji guilü ban shi, in: Hongqi, No. 5, 1980, pp. 31 et seqq.

Table 1   GROSS PRODUCTION VALUES BY SECTOR (in billions of
           Yuan), THEIR ANNUAL PERCENTAGE RATES OF GROWTH
           AND LIGHT INDUSTRY'S SHARE IN THE GROSS VALUE OF
           INDUSTRIAL PRODUCTION

	1978	%	1979	%	1980	%	1981	% (1982 Plan)
Agri-culture	146	8.6	158	2.7	163	5.7	172	4
Industry	423	8.5	459	8.7	499	4.1	519	4
Light industry	181	9.6	198	18.4	234	14.1	268	7
Heavy industry	243	7.7	261	1.4	265	-4.7	252	1
Light industry's share in the gross value of industrial production	42.7%		43.1%		46.9%		51.4%	

Sources: Communiqués 1978, 1979, 1980 and 1981 and Renmin Ribao,
          6.5.1982.(Figures have been rounded off.)

b)   Restructuring within individual sectors

58.   Analysis of branch structures and product ranges within individual
sectors shows that neither factories' demand for intermediate inputs nor
the population's demand for consumer goods is being satisfied at the
level that should be attainable in view of the available production potential and the economic power of the country. Great quantities of completely unwanted goods were being produced; for example, too many
iron and steel products were made, so that more than 10 million tonnes

of them are now lying unused in store. Other products for which there is great demand, such as bicycles, are simply not produced in sufficient quantities.[1]

These shortcomings are essentially due to fact that Chinese planners paid insufficient attention to shifts in the demand for industrial inputs and consumer goods resulting from changes in relationships between industries and in consumer's requirements during the development process and all too frequently rolled earlier investment programmes over fundamentally unchanged. Imbalances that occurred produced hardly any effect, for there was absolutely no economic pressure on the administrative authorities to react correctly and amend their plans accordingly. The enterprises, which could have helped iron out imbalances of their own accord by modifying their production programmes lacked the power of decision, the perception of market conditions and the necessary funds.

The authorities responsible for the development of the various branches of activity have been given concrete guidelines designed to bring production better into line with demand. At the same time, enterprises and producers' co-operatives have been given wider powers of decision and greater responsibility as an incentive to fine tune their production programmes to demand within the framework laid down by the state. The sections that follow examine the way in which the production mix has changed within heavy industry, light industry and agriculture over the last three years as a result of these measures and the prospects that may be expected in the light of the priorities that have been set.

Heavy industry

59. As stated above, the branches producing for the sector's own consumption are to be cut back. From the Chinese point of view these comprise chiefly the iron and steel industry and the engineering industry. By contrast, the expansion of capacity in the branches of heavy

1 Cf. YANG Jianbei, LI Xuefeng: The Relations between Agriculture, Light Industry and Heavy Industry in China, in: Social Sciences in China, Vol. 12, 1980, p. 188.

industry that manufacture producer goods required in light industry, agriculture and the transport sector is to continue.

60. Implementation of the intended investment cuts in the iron and steel industry was clearly no simple matter, as the very high annual rates of growth in steel production before 1981 testify; the rates were 34 per cent in 1978, still as high as 9 per cent in 1979 and 8 per cent in 1980. (In 1980 steel production came to 37 million tonnes.)[1]

61. The continuing increase in production in contradiction to the official development priorities is attributable largely to the start-up of plant that had been under construction long before the change in policy. However, even after 1978 new works were being built or existing plant extended, essentially because consensus had still not been reached among economic policymakers on implementation of the new development course. It was not until the end of 1980 that the forces critically disposed towards an expansion of steel production gained decisive influence within the leadership. Doubts were expressed about its catalytic effect on growth in the other branches of activity; indeed, it was even argued that the forced development of the steel industry would not stimulate but impede the growth of the other sectors of the economy as they would be deprived of urgently needed factors of production such as energy or transport. Moreover, it was pointed out that steel could hardly be in short supply when unused stocks ran to many millions of tonnes.

62. Furthermore, a review of a number of planned projects in the iron and steel industry brought to light serious planning and design errors that cast doubt upon their viability. This affected in particular the steel complex at Baoshan near Shanghai,[2] which was to have an annual production capacity of about 6 million tonnes. The project was to be constructed with foreign help, including the participation of German firms. At the end of 1980 it was first decided to halt construction and

---

1   Cf. Communiqué 1978, p. 25; Communiqué 1979, p. 32; and Renmin Ribao, 30.4.1981.

2   Cf. The China Business Review, January-February 1981, pp. 9 et seqq.

44

cancel the contracts with the foreign firms. Work was also stopped on other major schemes that were being constructed with foreign assistance; the Chinese appeared to be defaulting on foreign contracts worth billions of US dollars. The foreign contractors insisted on performance of the contracts or the payment of contractual penalties.

Cancellation of the contracts would have been very costly for China and the country's international standing as a reliable trading partner would have been seriously undermined. Moreover, a few members of the Chinese leadership had been personally involved in concluding some of the contracts. The end result was that China revised her decision to halt the projects; talk is now only of postponement. China intends to compensate the western firms for the losses incurred. According to official announcements, work on the projects will be resumed in two or three year's time. By then China wants to have more or less completed the restructuring of the economy so that she can devote her energies once again to major new projects, including those in heavy industry.

Some of the projects approved at the end of the seventies were badly planned, however, the Baoshan scheme, in particular, is regarded as a scandal by Chinese specialists because of its serious shortcomings. Neverthelses, such vast resources have already been invested in the project that the fear of an investment disaster swallowing many billion Yuan was enough to sway the economic policymakers in favour of continuation. Since then, emphasis is once again being placed on the positive aspects of the project - it is being said that it will embody the very latest technology.

63. For the time being, however, production cutbacks have been made in the steel sector. In 1981 steel production fell by 4 per cent and in 1982 it is to be reduced by the same percentage to 34 million tonnes.[1]

64. In some branches of engineering cuts were achieved more quickly than in the iron and steel sector. For example, the production of machine tools, hundreds of thousands of which were standing idle in facto-

1 Cf. Communiqué 1981; Renmin Ribao, 6.5.1982.

ries, was reduced by more than 23 per cent in 1979 compared with the previous year; in 1980 it was trimmed by a further 4 per cent and in 1981 by 23 per cent.[1] Nonetheless, there are still unresolved problems of adjustment in the industry. For instance, in 1980 electrical appliances and spare parts for them were still being produced in large quantities although there was absolutely no demand for them. Stocks of electrical equipment rose further and are now reported to have reached the fantastic value of 60 billion Yuan.[2]

65. The level of priority to be given to the agricultural machinery industry is still under discussion. In principle, the mechanisation of agricultural work is desirable, but there is now increasing awareness of the problems that it will bring in its train. These questions will be treated in greater detail in the section on agriculture (paragraph 77). In any case, the production of tractors was reduced dramatically in 1980 and 1981.[3]

66. The construction of new capacity in the chemical sector is continuing, although at a slightly slower pace since the beginning of 1981. The slowdown is due mainly to the fact that the production of crude oil, which is an important raw material for the chemical industry, has failed to expand as planned. In 1980 106 million tonnes of crude oil were produced, no more than in 1979. In 1981 production fell by 4.5 per cent to 101.2 million tonnes and further decline to 100 million tonnes in expected in 1982.[4]

67. As stated above (paragraph 53), energy is in such short supply that the existing industrial plant cannot be used to capacity. It is not only electricity that is lacking but also mineral oil and coal, with which China would also like to earn desperately needed foreign currency.

There are many reasons for the energy problems. First there is the lack of transport facilities and nationwide grid systems, so that it is

1 Cf. Communiqués 1979, 1980 and 1981.

2 Cf. Gongren Ribao, 17.4.1981.

3 Cf. Communiqués 1980 and 1981.

4 Cf. Communiqués 1980 and 1981; Renmin Ribao, 6.5.1981.

46

difficult to smooth out regional peaks in demand. The most important cause, however, is the wastage of energy in the widest sense. According to Chinese data the energy utilisation coefficient in China is 28 per cent; by comparison, the same source states that in Japan, for example, the coefficient is about 50 per cent.[1] The low level of energy efficiency is partly ascribable to the fact that enterprises have too little interest in energy conservation measures because of their close dependence on the state planning system and the specific production and consumption figures they are set. Moreover, the rapid expansion of production in heavy industry, especially iron and steel, entailed the swift growth of precisely those sectors and industries that have relatively high energy requirements. Above all, however, the process of modernisation that leads to the better utilisation of the factors of production has been very slow in China. Having previously pursued a growth policy oriented mainly towards widening the economy, China continued too long with the production of outdated equipment with relatively low energy utilisation coefficients. Few modern labour-saving and energy-efficient plant were installed.

Finally, the high consumption of energy can be traced back to China's dualistic economic structure. In the interests of improving facilities in rural areas, the establishment of traditional labour-intensive workshops in the villages has been encouraged as well as the creation of modern capital-intensive enterprises. This has created jobs in rural areas, improved the supply of industrial goods even in remote regions and minimised the social tensions that usually accompany industrialisation, as industry came to the country rather than farm workers having to move to the towns,[2] but the traditional or intermediate technologies employed make less efficient use of production factors and hence energy than do modern factories.[3]

1 Cf. XNA, 13.1.1980.

2 See for example KLENNER, Wolfgang: Ordnungsprinzipien im Industrialisierungsprozeß der VR China, loc. cit., pp. 329 et seqq.

3 Cf. SMIL, Vaclav: China's Energetics: A System Analysis, in: Chinese Economy Post-Mao. A Compendium of Papers, submitted to the Joint Economic Committee, Congress of the United States, Vol. 1, Policy and Performance, Washington 1978, pp. et seqq.

68. In the debate on the solution of the energy problems the view was expressed that the energy bottlenecks should be removed by rapidly expanding the production of energy. However, the opposite view was also put forward: instead of investing tens of billions of Yuan in stepping up energy production, it would be better to spend these sums on modernising antiquated plant. The present level of energy production would then be sufficient to meet industry's needs for many years and, as a bonus, the other factors of production would be used more economically, thus improving the country's international competitiveness.

In 1980 there was a trend towards first expanding the production of energy, but now there seems to be keener interest than before in modernising existing industrial plant. The path finally taken will probably lie somewhere between these two extremes.

69. The fact that investment in the energy sector generally affects production only in the long term will surely carry some weight in this regard. In 1979 and 1980 a considerable volume of capital, including some from abroad, was invested in expanding the coal, oil and electricity generating sectors. Even the greatly reduced investment budgets for 1981 and 1982 set aside substantial sums for the development of the energy sector. In spite of this, coal production barely increased (it rose from 618 million tonnes in 1978 to only 620 million in 1981; a reduction of 5 million tonnes is planned for 1982) and oil extraction even declined as it has not yet been possible to overcome the technical problems with the exploitation of new deposits. On the other hand, relatively high growth rates were achieved in the production of electricity, at least in 1979 and 1980, when it rose by just under 10 per cent and almost 7 per cent respectively. In 1981 it increased by just under 3 per cent and a similar rate of growth is envisaged in 1982.[1]

1 Cf. Communiqués 1979, 1980 and 1981; Renmin Ribao, 6.5.1982.

70. Provision was made for an expansion in the supply of goods from all branches of light industry. As a rule, there was no overcapacity here, in contrast to heavy industry, where goods to the value of billions of Yuan had been produced needlessly. On the contrary, demand for light industrial goods exceeded supply in practically all branches and many everyday requisites were obtainable only in exchange for coupons. In the few instances where goods proved difficult to sell, the problems were easily overcome by changing the product range or reducing the price, which the state often set at many times the cost.

71. No particular branches of light industry were accorded priority, but the growth rates achieved so far in two major spheres differ appreciably. Production increases were high mainly in sectors where intermediate inputs came from industry. Hence the annual rates of growth in the production of television sets came to more than 150 per cent in 1979, more than 80 per cent in 1980 and as much as 120 per cent in 1981. The manufacture of radio sets rose by almost 120 per cent in 1980 and by 35 per cent in 1981. It is now impossible to sell this vast output of radios at the set state price, which is now far too high in relation to demand, so that stocks of radios are steadily increasing. (The cumbersome planning machinery is obviously unable to decide on a swift price adjustment.) Remarkable annual growth rates of 30 per cent and more were also recorded in the production of bicycles, sewing machines, wrist watches and cameras in 1980 and 1981.

72. Rates of growth were markedly lower in branches of light industry that chiefly process agricultural products. The constraint here lies with agriculture, which has only limited scope to increase the production of the necessary raw materials such as cotton, sugar beet or oilseeds. As agriculture's ability to produce ever larger quantities of raw materials for light industry is still limited for the present in spite of the great efforts that have been made, manufacturers are turning increasingly to industrial substitutes. For example, emphasis is being placed on expand-

ing the production of artificial fibres (which totalled more than 500 000 tonnes in 1981), mainly by importing plant from abroad. [1]

Agriculture

73. Grain cultivation was previously at the centre of efforts to develop agriculture. Grain production played the same role in agriculture as steel in industry by constituting one of the so-called main chain links whose rapid development would, it was hoped, stimulate the entire economy. At the beginning of 1979, however, increasing support rallied to the view that excessive concentration on grain production might prevent agriculture's growth potential from being fully realised, as cereals would all to often be planted in soils and climates that would be much better suited to other crops. In order to make the best possible use of conditions in each locality, the government took appropriate measures to permit and encourage a diversification of agricultural production by the agricultural producers' co-operatives and, at a later stage in the economic reforms, by individual households.

74. There are no precise views on the desirable balance between the various types of agricultural activity. Nevertheless, the figure of 70 per cent of gross agricultural output recorded for grain production at the end of the seventies was considered to be far too high; it was pointed out that in some developed countries the cultivation of field crops constituted no more than 40 per cent of agricultural production (arable farming and animal husbandry). By the same token, the shares of the other types of farming were held to be far too low (paragraph 78). [2]

75. The debate on the most appropriate structure of agricultural production has still not reached its conclusion. Initially it was thought

1 Cf. Communiqués 1979, 1980 and 1981.
2 Cf. ISHIKAWA, Shigeru, loc. cit. p. 50; LÜ Lüping: loc. cit. p. 28; Jingji Guanli, No. 5, 1981, p. 15; The China Business Review, January-February 1980, p. 7.

that animal husbandry offered considerable growth potential. It was pointed out that China has vast areas of pasture (about 260 million hectares of usuable grassland) and it was thought that meat production could be expanded rapidly by applying suitable livestock methods. Now, however, the prospects are viewed with a little less optimism. It has been realised, for instance, that costly additional transport facilities or cold stores will be necessary if the supply of meat to the consumer is to be increased. Feed for the animals must also be guaranteed all the year round, which requires fodder that is not available at present.

Increases in grain production are therefore still regarded as extremely important in order to provide sufficient staple foodstuffs for a population that is once again rising at an annual rate of 1.4 per cent[1] (the return to the individual cultivation of the land led to an astonishingly rapid increase in the birth rate, as the numer of workers in the family assumed renewed importance). In principle, agricultural diversification will not be allowed to jeopardise grain production.

76.   In any event, agriculture is to be subject to fewer state planning directives than previously. The scale and structure of agricultural production, in other words the extent of diversification, are to be decided mainly by the collective and by the individual farmer.

In recent years the state has eased the financial constraints on agricultural producers' co-operatives and households by raising the purchasing prices for agricultural products, granting tax concessions, reducing the prices of industrial goods used in agriculture and providing loans on favourable terms. It has thus improved the financial conditions for the optimum adaptation of agricultural production to the climate, the soil and demand.

Other measures have also been taken. A start has been made with the construction of slaughterhouses and cold stores to which both co-operatives and individuals can deliver their animals (at the end of 1980 they

1   Cf.   Communiqué 1981.

totalled about 800, of which 260 had been completed in that year a-
lone).[1] Private agriculture was encouraged by increasing the permitted
area of private plots to 15 per cent of the co-operative's total land
area[2] and authorising private markets. There are now more than 40 000
such markets at which co-operatives and individuals sell their produce.[3]

77. It is still uncertain to what extent producer's co-operatives and
agricultural households geared towards income maximisation will be
interested in the purchase of additional tractors or other agricultural
machinery. Stocks of medium and heavy tractors and hand tillers were
still rising until 1981; however, production was cut drastically and the
utilisation rate of plant producing agricultural machinery was well below
capacity. In 1980 22 per cent fewer medium and heavy tractors were
produced than in the previous year, and in 1981 the decline came to 46
per cent.[4]

The use of tractors is clearly far less profitable than Chinese planners
have assumed hitherto. This is borne out by several pieces of evidence.
For example, in 1978 only 70 per cent of all available tractors were
serviceable[5] owing to insufficient maintenance, which could be blamed
as much on a lack of interest as on technical problems. Even the serviceable machines were not always fully utilised, because the marginal
cost of fuel and other expenses often exceeded the marginal earnings.
From the point of view of the individual enterprise, it is often still
cheaper to use manual labour, which is available in abundance. From
the point of view of the economy as a whole there are also employment
problems due to the fact that there are no suitable new jobs for farmers
displaced as a result of mechanisation. For this reason, efforts to increase agricultural output will concentrate first on raising yields per
hectare in ways that do not cause a shakeout of labour. It appears that

1   Cf.   Business America, 3.5.1982.
2   Cf.   Guangming Ribao, 7.4.1981.
3   Cf.   Jingji Guanli, No. 5, 1981, p. 12.
4   Cf.   Communiqués 1980 and 1981.
5   Cf.   Communiqué 1978.

this approach still contains considerable growth potential that can be released by the appropriate use of suitable inputs.[1]

78. As the available data on the composition of agricultural output show, efforts to develop and diversify the sector have not been without success. The gross production value of the sector has grown by several percentage points each year. Grain production, which increased from 305 million tonnes in 1978 to 325 million tonnes in 1981, declined as a proportion of gross agricultural output from almost 70 per cent at the end of the seventies to 64 per cent in 1981 while the share of forestry rose from about 3 per cent to 4.1 per cent and that of private agriculture increased from 11.9 per cent to 14.3 per cent over the same period.[2]

C   Imports and the use of foreign capital

79. A further important set of measures under the new development strategy relates to the import of modern plant and technology in order to remove bottlenecks and increase overall productivity. The section that follows will attempt to ascertain whether the expected development effects actually materialised. As China's foreign trade activities will be examined in detail in the second chapter of this study, we shall consider only imports of plant in this context and only in relation to the question whether they have so far given the expected boost to growth.

The planned flood of imports of plant and technology occurred in 1979 and 1980. In 1979 such imports totalled about 3.6 billion Yuan, almost three times the figure for 1978.[3] In 1980 there was a further substantial increase; the import value of complete plant alone rose by more than 100 per cent to 3.7 billion Yuan.[4] In addition to this there were

1 Cf. FANG Yuan: Woguo nongye xiandaihua de jiben renwu yingshi tigao danwei mianji chanliang, in: Jingji Yanjiu, No. 3, 1980, pp. 3 et seqq.
2 Cf. Communiqués 1978, 1979, 1980 and 1981.
3 Cf. Communiqué 1979.
4 Cf. Renmin Ribao, 30.4.1981.

imports of equipment and technology worth several billion Yuan. Probably more than half of the plant and technology worth US-$ 11 billion imported since the beginning of the seventies was shipped in 1979 and 1980 alone.[1]

China took up foreign loans to the value of several billion dollars in order to finance her imports (paragraph 147). In addition, up to the end of 1980 China availed herself of foreign capital worth well over US-$ 2 billion under joint ventures in the broadest sense and compensation agreements (paragraphs 155 et seqq.). This does not include equipment and plant brought in by French and Japanese oil companies under co-operation agreements for the development of offshore oilfields.

80. According to the information available, serious problems arose with many of the complete plant imported on normal commercial terms (paragraph 62). In some cases completion was considerably delayed because the separate construction phases where badly co-ordinated. Once the plant had been brought into operation there were all too often difficulties with the supply of the necessary inputs. There was also a shortage of trained Chinese staff. As a result, only a small part of the production capacity of many factories built with foreign help could be utilised. In certain large plant the capacity utilisation rate was well below 50 per cent and their productivity was correspondingly poor.

81. The import programme therefore came under fierce attack. Some Chinese authors even went so far as to state that the import of complete plant had not only wasted vast sums of money but had also delayed modernisation. In view of these criticisms, there are many indications that the plant imported at the end of the seventies far exceeded the Chinese economy's ability to absorb capital and that the hoped-for productivity gains and development effects did not materialise in spite of the foreign currency spent and loans taken up.[2]

---

1 Cf. CHEN Huiqin: Jishu yinjin de fangxiang bixu zhuanbian, in: Jingji Guanli, No. 4, 1981, pp. 22 et seqq.

2 Cf. CHEN Huiqin, loc. cit.

82. As fairly similar problems could be expected with some of the large factories ordered in 1978 and 1979 - in 1978 alone orders were placed for plant worth over 6 billion Yuan[1] - the government took the logical step. As explained above (paragraph 62), the supply contracts were first cancelled, then the projects were reinstated but construction was postponed for a few years. The postponement was partly due to the fact that the most important of these projects related to the expansion of the iron and steel industry and petrochemicals and that after the development strategy and expectations concerning a rapid increase in oil production had been revised there seemed little point in pushing rapidly ahead with them. Moreover, budgetary resources and foreign exchange worth tens of billions of Yuan would have been committed for years to come and would not have been available to develop the consumer goods sector and to modernise existing plant.

It is hoped that decisive progress with sectoral restructuring will be achieved in the next two or three years; work will then begin on the postponed large-scale projects for which contracts have already been concluded with foreign suppliers. For the present a large proportion of the funds available, including foreign exchange, are to be devoted to the modernisation programme (paragraphs 42 and 43). However, the modernisation of industry as a whole is viewed as a long-term undertaking, so that the financing requirement will remain very high for quite some time. Resumption of work on the major projects could therefore lead to a shortage of foreign exchange, but in all probability China will have no difficulty in covering this by raising loans in the West. It will be much more important for China to ensure that the projects are correctly designed and well suited to the prevailing conditions so that they are viable.

D   The raising of incomes

83. A brief explanation of the structure of the labour force will provide greater insight into the income measures that have been taken.

1   Cf. Beijing Rundschau, No. 20, 1980, p. 22.

There are about 400 million income recipients, of whom a quarter are workers and employees;[1] these are on the state payroll and receive fixed wages. The remaining 300 million are employed in agriculture or in small enterprises run by agricultural producers' collectives.[2] (A new element since the Cultural Revolution are the private workers, who run small repair businesses or shops. At the end of 1981 they totalled 1.1 million.)

Approximately three-quarters of the workers and employees are employed by state entities such as manufacturing enterprises, trading corporations, administrative bodies or schools, and the remainder work in municipal enterprises run on a co-operative basis. Some 270 million of the rural workers earn their living as farmers in agricultural producers' co-operatives and about 30 million work in the rural workshops[3] numbering almost 1.5 million run by rural producers' co-operatives. Unlike those of workers and employees, their incomes are determined by the level of net profits.

84. The state took the following measures to increase the incomes of workers and employees:

a.   The wages of selected groups of workers and employees were raised in stages. Since staff in the education system and in the health sector also received wage increases at the beginning of 1982, almost all workers and employees have enjoyed a raise.

b.   Bonuses have been paid in most industrial, trading and transport enterprises to reward increases in performance.[4] They are generally financed from retained operating profits. A uniform system of profit-

1   Cf.   Renmin Ribao, 30.4.1981.

2   Cf.   LI Long, LU Nan: Tantan   gongnongye pin jiage de jiandaocha, in: Hongqi, No. 6, p. 48.

3   Cf.   XNA, 17.5.1981.

4   Cf.   SUN Zhen: Qiye jiangli zhidu de jige wenti, in: Hongqi, No. 10, 1981, pp. 46 et seqq.;   see also: Yi tiaozheng wei zhongxin, nuli gaohao gongye shengchan he jiaotong yunshu, in: Hongqi, No. 8, 1981, p. 4.

sharing and bonuses does not yet exist; some enterprises may retain part of their overall profit and pay out a proportion of this in bonuses, while others receive a given percentage of their target profit and a generally larger share of any profits in excess of their plan target (paragraph 101). Under a further scheme enterprises share in profit growth and are permitted to pay out a certain proportion as bonuses. Other profitsharing schemes and bonus systems are being tried out; for example, in some enterprises bonuses are paid if the consumption of energy and raw materials remains below certain norms.

In 1978 bonuses averaged 10-12 percent of the wage bill in enterprises that were permitted to pay performance supplements. The proportion has now risen slightly and the sum total has increased sharply because bonuses are now paid in practically all enterprises.

c. All workers and employees were paid a cost-of-living increase of 5 Yuan (just under 10 per cent of average earnings). This is intended to compensate for the increase in the prices of important consumer goods that has occurred since 1979.

85. As a result of the across-the-board wage increases, bonuses and cost-of-living increases the average wage of all workers and employees rose form 614 Yuan per annum in 1978 to 772 Yuan in 1981, an increase of 25.7 per cent in nominal income. In real terms, however, the rise was smaller; if allowance is made for the officially announced increase in the cost-of-living, the increase in real incomes works out at just under 12 per cent. [1]

86. In order to create the financial conditions for an increase in rural incomes, in 1979 the state increased the purchasing price for the grain quotas that farmers are obliged to sell to the government by 20 per cent and that for quantities over and above the supply requirement by as much as 50 per cent. The state also paid higher prices for most

1 Cf. Communiqués 1978 and 1981.

other agricultural products, so that the index of state purchasing prices rose by 38.5 per cent between 1978 and 1981.[1]

The government also provided scope for improvements in incomes from the costs side by reducing the prices of important industrial inputs used in agriculture. Specific incomes policy measures were also taken; taxes on certain forms of agricultural activity were reduced and subsidies were granted to a number of regions that are particularly poor or have suffered natural disasters. Another positive influence was the fact that farmers were virtually freed from planning directives and could now grow whatever they considered would provide them with a living and maximise their incomes.

87.   The overall result of these measures was that average incomes per head of the rural population (not per person employed!) derived from work on the collective rose from 74 Yuan in 1978 to 85.9 Yuan in 1980.[2] Earnings from the cultivation of private plots come on top of this; no overall data are available, but the findings of a sample survey that income from this source more than doubled between 1978 and 1981 to stand at 84.5 Yuan[3] seem to indicate that the highest increases in income occurred in this field.

(During the Cultural Revolution private work was not well regarded, as it was often done at the expense of work within the collective. All that was needed for this activity to flourish was for the government to permit private work and authorise private markets at which small private producers could sell their produce.)

88.   The question arises whether the various measures to raise the wages of workers and employees and to increase the incomes of the rural population were such as would generate the expected growth effects. For this to happen it would be essential that more goods could be bought with the additional income. The growth in incomes should

1 Cf.   Communiqués 1979 and 1981.

2 Cf.   Communiqués 1978 and 1979;   Renmin Ribao, 30.4.1981.

3 Cf.   Xinhua Yuebao, No. 1, 1980, p. 103.

therefore have been matched by expansion in the consumer goods sector. As demonstrated above, the supply of consumer goods could not be increased as quickly as the economic policymakers had expected or to the extent 'anticipated' by wage increases. Production fell short of actual demand, and the result was inflation. [1]

It is not easy to obtain an accurate picture of the rate of price increases. According to official figures average retail prices rose by 5.8 per cent in 1979 and by 6 per cent in 1980. The cost-of-living is reported to have increased by 7.5 per cent in 1980 and the prices of so-called additional foodstuffs by 13.8 per cent. These inflation rates do not reflect "concealed" price increases (poor quality goods were sold as first-class items or the weight of goods in packets was reduced), which probably pushed the "actual" inflation rate into double figures in 1979 and 1980; [2] the rate of price increase does not appear to have slowed down until 1981. [3]

Hence a considerable part of the increase in incomes was eroded by inflation, so that the expected positive effects of increases in incomes may have been nullified and the support for the new policy that may have initially won may have been dissipated. However, the awareness that "something was happening" and that incomes could be increased by raising performances might possibly have been more important. This attitude was probably more prevalent in rural areas, where greater individual effort led to visible increases in incomes. (Another point was the fact that farmers are less affected by price increases as they supply some of their own needs.) In urban areas such vitalising effects might have stemmed from the payment of bonuses on condition, of course, that the payments were actually linked to increases in output, which was not always the case; firstly, the level of factory profits from which

---

1 In 1979 purchasing power is reported to have increased by 20 per cent but the supply of goods by only 15 per cent. In 1980 the corresponding rates of increase are said to have been 18.7 per cent and 13.3 per cent respectively. Cf. LI Long: Guanche tiaozheng fangzheng da li fazhan xiaofeipin shengchan, in: Jingji Yanjiu, No. 5, 1981, p. 10.

2 Cf. Ta Kung Pao, 30.4. - 6.5.1981.

3 Cf. Communiqué 1981.

bonuses were paid often had little to do with plant performance (for example, profits could be low in spite of great efforts on the part of the work force if planning deficiencies caused shortages of materials), and secondly bonuses were often paid more or less indiscriminately to the entire work force because it was not possible to record individual performances accurately.[1]

2)   Organisational measures

89. In accordance with the new organisational policy guidelines (paragraphs 24-32), relations within the economic administration between central government and lower administrative levels were modified. In addition, the position of enterprises in relation to the economic authorities was strengthened.

A   Decentralisation within the economic administration

90. The main purpose of decentralisation was to give the provincial administrations greater powers and provide them with financial resources of their own. Some degree of decentralisation had frequently been regarded as desirable in view of the size of some provinces (for example, Sichuan has more than 100 million inhabitants and eight other provinces have populations well in excess of 40 million), their linguistic distinctions, their historic particularities and in some cases their considerable economic power. In fact, however, far-reaching decentralisation had never come about because of the central government's recurrent fear that some provinces would become too independent and could easily take over tasks that it had no intention of relinquishing. Hence during various decentralisation phases provinces obtained their own financial resources, but they were not empowered to take economic decisions on their own initiative. Even these hesitant advances were later countermanded. In practice, almost every year responsibilities and financial resources were renegotiated between the central government and the

1 Cf. SUN Zhen: loc. cit.; Yi tiaozheng wei zhongxin ..., loc. cit.

provinces, including the centrally administered municipalities of Beijing, Shanghai and Tianjin which are treated as provinces for administrative purposes, with the central government having the final say over the responsibilities and resources of the provinces. It was therefore impossible for the provinces to plan their revenue, expenditure and building projects over the long term.

91. This is precisely the aim of the administrative reforms that have been carried out since the end of the seventies,[1] whereby as an experiment a few selected provinces are to receive a portion of their revenues, the rate being set individually for each province and remaining constant for several years. They will be largely free to use their own funds as they see fit and they can retain unspent amounts. (The provinces previously received precise allocations for their projects. Whatever they did not spend had to be transferred to the central government, so that as a rule they had no interest in making savings.) In this way the provinces involved can estimate their revenue over many years and plan accordingly.

92. The process of reform was begun in 1976. In the province of Jiangsu, the government abolished the previous system of finance which distinguished between planned revenue and revenue in excess of the plan target, with the provinces receiving a relatively large part of the latter but very little of the former. This had led the provinces to keep the plan figures for their revenue as low as possible in order to maximise their own receipts at the expense of the central government. It was soon evident that the new approach, which allowed the province to retain a given share of total revenue, produced good economic results, as the province's receipts (and those of the central government) were still rising at a time when the receipts of practically all other provinces were falling because of economic difficulties.

93. More far-reaching reforms were soon devised in order to give provinces various means of increasing their revenues. Under these schemes

1 Cf. XUE Muqiao: Jingji guanli tizhi gaige wenti, in: Hongqi No. 8, 1979, pp. 16 et seqq.; ZHU Fulin, XIANG Huaicheng: Dui gaige caizheng tizhi de yixie kanfa, in: Jingji Guanli, No. 5, 1979, pp. 16 et seqq.

provinces will no longer receive a fixed share of their total revenue but differing proportions from the most important source of revenue, i.e. industrial and commercial consolidated tax (a kind of turnover tax), and from enterprises' profits (these produce in equal proportions well over 80 per cent of state revenue).

In 1980 this system was introduced on a trial basis in about half the provinces, but not yet in Jiangsu or the centrally administered municipalities. The shares of taxes and profits differ from one province to another; the percentages for industrial and commercial consolidated tax range from 0 per cent to 88 per cent and those for profits between 48.7 per cent and 100 per cent. The provinces' shares in profits are high (in some cases absolute) in order to motivate them to reduce costs and increase turnover. On the other hand, the central government receives a larger share of industrial and commercial consolidated tax, which has shown relatively stable growth over the years.

94. The provinces Guangdong and Fujian were given special status; these provinces, which are also in a special position with regard to the determination of their external trade relations (paragraph 196), must pay only a fixed annual sum to the central government. They are permitted to retain all revenue in excess of this amount and to use it as they see fit. They thus have greater fiscal independence than the other provinces.

95. The authorities also wish to extend the principles governing relations between the central government and the provinces to those between the province and the districts and municipalities of which they are composed. For example, the province of Jiangsu now allows most of its regional administrative units to receive differing shares of the revenue.

96. The shares of central government, provinces and their subordinate administrative units are based essentially on their budgets for 1978 or 1979. This fundamentally perpetuates the income ratios then prevailing between central government and the regions and between the various

62

regions themselves. Regions that were at a relative disadvantage in 1978 or 1979 therefore remain in an unfavourable position in the years that follow. Vice versa, regions that came off relatively well in 1978 or 1979 stand a good chance of further increasing their revenue. This could marginally accentuate the existing regional disparities.

The authorities accept that blemish, however. In the interest of stimulating performances more strongly,[1] the additional revenue of high-income regions will no longer be creamed off when it exceeds a certain level. By the same token, low-revenue provinces will not receive as much support as in the past. Some financial assistance will continue to be given under vertical and horizontal revenue equalisation arrangements, but the authorities will no longer seek to place all regions on an equal financial footing, which would penalise good economic performance and reward failure.

97. The administrative reforms ran into difficulties soon after their introduction. The raising of workers' and employees' wages by the state (at the expense of operating profits and hence state revenue from profits) and the increase in the prices of agricultural products (which made state subsidies necessary because the selling prices of certain produce such as rice remained constant) caused central government revenue to fall and expenditure to rise.[2] The central government therefore tried to extract more funds from the provinces that it was due to receive under the formulae that had been previously laid down. It did this partly "according to the system" by selling interest-bearing Treasury bonds to the regional administrations. However, this did not raise enough, so that in spite of the fact that the rates of revenue-sharing were actually valid for several years the state demanded increased funds from the provinces. Such arbitrary adjustments may

1 See for example LING Chen: Shilun caitizhi gaige de zuoyong jiqi wanshan de tujing, in: Caizheng Yanjiu, No. 4, 1982, pp. 1 et seqq.

2 Cf. LI Chengrui: Caizheng, xindai pingheng yu guomin jingji de zonghe pingheng, in: Jingji Yanjiu, No. 3, 1981, p. 6; XNA, 30.6. 1979 and 31.8.1980; Beijing Rundschau, No. 12, 1981, p. 24; see also HISHIDA, Masaharu: State Finance and Financial Reforms, in: JETRO, China Newsletter, October 1980, pp. 15. et seqq.

easily wipe out the stimulus to improved performance, as the provinces view them as a reversion to the previous practice.

98.   The reforms are also beset by other problems attributable to the fact that there is still no clear concept for the division of responsibilities between the central government and the regions nor any precise idea which tasks should be undertaken by the economic administration and which by enterprises. Admittedly, it has been decided in principle that investment shall no longer be the exclusive preserve of government; enterprises must increasingly borrow the necessary funds from the banks or generate them themselves. However, it remains to be clarified whether in future the state should confine itself to financing infrastructure projects in the broadest sense or should also finance selected projects in industry and trade. The development of a rational system of finance will depend on the answers to these questions.

B   Expansion of enterprises' freedom of action

99.   The creation of relatively independent enterprise units with extensive powers of decision over production, procurement and sales was at the heart of the organisational reforms. Certain guiding principles were followed (paragraphs 26-32), but as with decentralisation within the economic administration there was no overall concept defined in every detail.

The reforms are intended as a long-term process in which experience must first be gained. The authorities want to see how enterprises behave if they have a share in profits and have some degree of independence in matters of production, procurement and sales and they want to await the macro-economic effects that will ensue.

a.   Profit sharing and the creation of entrepreneurial freedom of action

100. The industrial reforms were launched in 1978 in the province of Sichuan.[1] Initially a small number of selected enterprises no longer had to transfer their total profits to the authorities and the bureaux allocated no more funds to them for specific purposes (e.g. product development, technical improvements or job protection measures); instead, they were allowed to retain a set portion of their profits. As a rule, the share was calculated in such a way that the enterprise would be left with a sum equivalent to the funds it received from the adminis- tration the previous year. Hence the companies involved were not placed at any financial advantage. The point of the exercise was that the percentage share would remain constant for several years. This aroused the enterprises' interest in raising profits by their own efforts and thus increasing their own receipts.

101. Within a short while profit-sharing was extended to a large number of enterprises throughout the country. Various procedures were used. Initially the authorities fell back on the conventional distinction between profits in excess of the plan to calculate the portion to be retained. Enterprises received differing proportions of each component of profits, with the share of plan profits (usually about 5 per cent) being ap- preciably lower than that of profits in excess of the plan (generally about 20 per cent). This had the desired effect of encouraging the enterprises to raise turnover above the planned level and keep costs below those budgeted in the plan. One disadvantage of such a profit- sharing system, however, was that it increased the enterprises' interest in keeping their plan targets, and in particular their plan profits, as low as possible in the annual negotiations with the authorities; they were able to do so by not revealing the full extent of their production capacity or their ability to cut costs.

---

1   Cf. Renmin Ribao, 4.4.1980 and 9.5.1980;   REN Tao: Sichuan bai ge shidian qiye su jian chengxiao de yuanyin he zai?, in: Jingji Guanli, No. 12, 1979, pp. 6 et seqq.; KLENNER, Wolfgang: Market-Economic Experiments, in: Intereconomics, January-February 1981, pp. 43 et seqq.

In order to prevent this, the distinction between plan profits and excess profits was abandoned in most firms for the purposes of allocating profits. In some firms the annual profit is compared with that of the so-called base year (generally 1978 or 1979). Their share of additional profits (amounts in excess of the base profits) is larger than that portion equal to the level of the base year. Hence some enterprises receive a 5 per cent share of profits up to the equivalent for the base year and 20 per cent of any profits over and above this. In other enterprises no distinction is made between different components of profits, so that they may retain a fixed percentage of the total.

In addition, there is a relatively small number of enterprises that only have to pay taxes,[1] which might be seen as the first step towards a uniform system of taxation without the transfer of profits. The idea behind it is as follows: it makes no sense to have uniform rates of profits tax for all enterprises in view of the present distortions in the price system. In present circumstances high profits are hardly an indication that a firm has performed efficiently; as a rule, they are merely the result of prices having been set well above unit costs by the state.[2] For this reason the authorities want to levy a so-called regulatory tax in order first to cream off those components of profits that have nothing to do with the performance of the enterprise but derive solely from price distortions. The objective is to achieve balance between the various ways in which sectors and enterprises can make profits. Profits net of regulatory tax will then be subject to a uniform rate of profits tax. The regulatory tax can be gradually reduced as price controls are progressively removed and price distortions disappear

---

1 Although in principle the deduction of profits described above also amounts to the taxation of profits, the distinction is to be found in Chinese literature (paragraph 112).

2 Cf. HISHIDA, Masaharu, loc. cit., p. 21.

owing to the adjustment of prices to supply and demand. All that would then remain would be the uniform profits tax.[1]

102. The share of profits that the reformed enterprises can retain amounts to more than 10 per cent of their total profits.[2] The retained resources are used in accordance with official guidelines for the payment of bonuses (bonus fund), for raising the level of company welfare (welfare fund) and for developing production (production fund), in other words for matters in which the works management and the labour force have a direct interest. Profit maximisation therefore constitutes the main business objective of the reformed enterprises and influences the production programme, the marketing of products and the procurement of inputs. In all these fields the state has given the reformed enterprises greater freedom of action than before. (Nonetheless, powers of decision have not been widened to the same extent for all reformed enterprises. Those that manufacture items considered to be of low importance for the economy have been given wider powers of decision than enterprises producing economically important goods; see paragraphs 26-28).

103. Hence reformed enterprises are no longer obliged to arrange production to meet plan targets, or at least not exclusively so. They can either determine their production programme independently or, if they receive mandatory plan directives, they can produce "excess quantities" and/or extend their range of goods.

104. State contracts requiring firms to supply specified quantities to the state "allocation system"[3] now only apply to products considered to

1 Enterprises that pay regulatory taxes and profits taxes are liable to other taxes as well. Apart from industrial and commercial consolidated tax, which is levied on all enterprises, they also have to pay a capital investment tax or "usage fee" on the procurement value of plant. This is equivalent to interest on the national capital that has been placed at the enterprise's disposal. They also pay land taxes, taxes on their fleets of lorries, etc.

2 Cf. Renmin Ribao, 29.5.1981.

3 See for example XUE Muqiao: Tantan shengchan ziliao liutong wenti, in: Wuzi Guanli, No. 1, 1980, pp. 1 et seqq. and LI Kaixin: An shangpin yuanze zuzhi shengchan ziliao de liutong, in: Wuzi Guanli, No. 1, 1980, pp. 7 et seqq.

be of especial importance for the economy as a whole, such as building timber, cement or certain sorts of steel. If they manufacture other goods they are free to sell their output to other buyers as well. In order to help firms open up new "distribution channels" parallel to the state "allocation system", which was tantamount to a monopoly, ministries and regional bureaux organise fairs at which suppliers and potential buyers of specific goods can meet. Enterprises are also encouraged to sell products as agents of other firms or to set up their own marketing organisations. In principle it should be possible to sell goods throughout the country irrespective of regional boundaries and also to export them. Nevertheless, foreign trade relations are still largely under the control of state foreign trade bodies (see Chapter II).

105. The reformed enterprises have also been given greater latitude in the procurement of inputs. It is now rare for them to be allocated centrally planned factors of production by the state "allocation system" direct. Instead, they receive so-called certificates of entitlement (allocated on the basis of their production plans) which enable them to obtain the relevant factors of production from branches of the state "allocation system" or manufacturers of their choice on mutually acceptable terms. Production factors that are not centrally planned can be obtained anywhere without special formalities. As with the marketing of their products, regional boundaries should no longer hold any significance. In principle it should also be possible to obtain inputs direct from abroad, but in practice this facility has been granted to only a very small number of enterprises (paragraph 209).

106. The changes in the procurement and marketing system designed to make enterprises compete against one another as suppliers and consumers are reinforced by the deregulation of prices in stages since the end of the seventies. This has enabled many enterprises (such as those producing simple household articles) to use price as well as product quality or service as a parameter of competition. Other enterprises such as manufacturers of car tyres or electric fans, may set their prices themselves but only within limits fixed by administration. This has been done partly to avoid excessive price movements, which could have un-

desirable repercussions on incomes or the allocation of resources, and partly to bring prices more closely into line with supply shortages.

By contrast, the state continues to set uniform prices for goods that are considered especially important for the economy, such as basic foodstuffs, petrol, coal or electricity, because of their great significance for income distribution. (In some cases the yardstick used is the industry's average unit cost plus a profit margin or less any state subsidy applicable; see paragraph 31.) This does hamper the formation of scarcity prices, even in "free" sectors, as their intermediate inputs include goods with administered prices, for example.

107. Finally, reforms in the financing of investment have given enterprises greater freedom in their decision-making but also greater responsibility.[1] Hitherto, the fixed capital of state enterprises and that part of their working capital that is required throughout the year to ensure smooth production was provided from the budget without any repayment obligation (paragraph 29). Loans were granted only if an additional capital requirement arose - as a result of seasonal fluctuations in production, for example. Under the previous system it was very difficult for enterprises to obtain capital, but once it had been provided there were no economic mechanisms to ensure that they used it economically and efficiently.

In order to change this situation, in 1979 the authorities began to provide selected enterprises in Sichuan with capital only in the form of loans. The enterprises involved no longer had to cover their capital requirements by applying for finance to the administration, which in appropriate cases would instruct the banks to provide outright grants of funds. Instead, they went direct to the banks, from which they received loans if they could convince them that their plans were viable and that they could repay the loan and if they could prove that the projects were "materially and technically" feasible, in other words that their supplies of the necessary inputs were assured. As this procedure had the desired result that additional capital was requested only after

1 See for example ZHAO Xi'an: Lun yinhang zai jihua zhong de tiaojie zuoyong, in: Zhongguo Jinrong, No. 10, 1982, pp. 18 et seqq.

detailed viability studies had been made and the enterprises had en-
sured that the repayment of the principal and the payment of interest
would pose no problems, this system of finance was extended to enterprises throughout the country in 1980.

Although the building of new factories and large-scale projects by
existing enterprises will still be financed out of the budget, the modernisation of plant must now as a rule be financed by borrowing. In 1980
the banks lent a total of 6.3 billion Yuan for such schemes; the People's
Bank alone has set aside 7.8 billion Yuan for loans in 1982, of which 25
per cent will be used in the modernisation of plant in light industry, 20
per cent in the modernisation of engineering enterprises and 4 per cent
for energy saving measures. This does not include lending by the other
banks, such as the Agricultural Bank, the Construction Bank and the
Bank of China, for which plan data had not been published at the time
of writing. [1]

The state still determines the volume of credit and the sectoral break-
down of credit utilisation, but in the past the banks have not always
abided by such state directives, particularly if the deposits (from
enterprises and individuals) from which they could finance lending
exceeded the credit lines set for them. The result was that the banking
sector as a whole exceeded the volume of credit the economy could
support, thus causing excessive growth in the money supply and in the
demand for capital goods.

b.   Continuation and revision of the reforms

108. By 1981 the reforms giving enterprises greater freedom in procurement and marketing and a share in their profits had been extended to
more than 6 000 of the largest and most profitable enterprises.

1   Cf. Far Eastern Economic Review, 28.5.1982.

In mid 1981 it was decided not to increase the number of enterprises involved for the time being, as the authorities first wish to evaluate the reforms, which are described as experimental. Schemes that do not seem beneficial are to be terminated, while those that look promising are to be continued, improved and, if appropriate, extended to other enterprises in the future.

109. No detailed reform programme has yet been drawn up for the years immediately ahead, but it is known how the reforms are viewed in principle and the direction the authorities wish to take.

The outcome of the enterprise reforms is considered on the whole to be positive. It is pointed out that the production of many goods rose as a result of the reforms, that in many cases the range of products was extended, services improved and costs reduced. However, undesirable side-effects have also been noted. In order to maximise profits, enterprises "abused" the de facto monopoly situation they often enjoy as a result of the underdevelopment of the transport sector or the parochial policies of regional administrations. Hence they raised their prices[1] but did not increase production, while at the same time letting quality and service deteriorate. The co-existence of a "free" sector alongside the state sector also gave rise to problems. In order to maximise their profits enterprises manufactured mainly products on which they could earn a large markup, but these were not necessarily the goods the state was interested in having produced. For example, the state pursues a low-price policy for products that it considers to be of particular importance for the population; enterprises oriented towards maximum profits are therefore no longer interested in producing them.

110. Many of the problems that have arisen are attributed to the fact that since the introduction of market elements into planned economy the control mechanisms of central quantity planning are no longer fully operational but institutional conditions are not yet such that the decisions of individual enterprises lead to an optimum for the economy as a whole. However, the authorities shrink from rapidly creating the con-

1 Cf. Renmin Ribao, 24.8.1982.

ditions that constitute a "socialist market economy". They still do not know how the economic and institutional requirements of a workable competitive economy can be comfortably reconciled with the conditions and aims peculiar to socialist China. It is also feared that a hasty removal of price controls will have adverse effects on income distribution and resource allocation. Finally, the authorities are not yet confident that plant managers, who were hardly accustomed to think in economic terms or to act independently in the past, can perform the relatively complicated tasks incumbent upon them in a more competitive economy or that administrators can quickly come to grips with the completely new tools for exercising indirect control over the economy. In view of these uncertainties and risks, the economic policymakers prefer gradual solutions that do not exclude even a temporary recentralisation in certain fields rather than radical changes.

111. Hence China is cautiously feeling her way through a series of measures towards a system based on market forces, but one that suits the conditions and aims of Chinese society. This includes the creation of a law of contract governing the rights and duties arising from contracts between economically independent entities,[1] the establishment of rules of competition and the provision of commercial training for factory managers. In order to create the institutional framework in which the investment decisions of individual enterprises produce beneficial results for the economy as a whole, it is intended that an independent central bank will be founded to monitor the capability of the commercial banks. In order to give firms still more independence, consideration is being given to increasing their financial freedom still further by expanding their share of profits that they may use to improve and enlarge plant and for certain factory welfare schemes such as the construction of canteens, sanitary facilities or even apartments. By contrast, the share earmarked for bonuses is to be reduced; it is believed that if bonuses are linked more closely to performance the amounts paid can be cut without reducing the incentives. (In the past bonuses were all too often paid across the board, and were thus not tied to performance.)

1 Cf. Renmin Ribao, 22.6.1981.

The aim of giving enterprises greater financial opportunities is also served by the intended increase in the rates of depreciation allowances, which are still extremely low at present. The full write-off period for most plant is 25 years or longer; more over, enterprises can retain only part of the amounts written off (about one half) to finance plant replacement themselves. The remainder goes to the relevant industry bureaux, which use the funds in accordance with broader criteria. (This depreciation system was designed for a development policy geared mainly towards the creation of new production capacity. It has led to a serious absolescence of the economy's industrial base, which has long been criticised by many Chinese economists.)

The failure to raise depreciation rates up to now has been caused primarily by fear of a decline in state revenue which would have necessitated cutting the funds for new projects. Higher rates of depreciation increase enterprises' prime costs and, at unchanged prices, reduce profits. The modernisation of existing plant has now been given high priority. Moreover, as this entails investment decisions that should mainly be taken by enterprises, the large-scale absorption of plants' earnings is no longer particularly desirable. Under these circumstances the advocates of higher depreciation rates have been able to make their voices heard. A gradual increase to an average of about 10 per cent is under dicussion.

In regard to modernisation, the question arises whether productivity could not be increased more quickly by importing foreign machinery than by using equipment manufactured in China (paragraph 45). The answer to this question does not depend on technical factors alone. It is conceivable that the advantages of western machinery do not always materialise in the conditions pertaining in Chinese enterprises. In cases where the import of plant seems sensible after all the relevant questions have been considered, the enterprise involved should at least have a say in the decision. However, this presupposes that they have a knowledge of the products available on the world market, either because they have received the necessary information from Chinese trade organisations or because foreign firms have visited them in China to display their products.

112. Other movements towards reforms have slowed down or even come to a temporary standstill. For example, the impetus of the attempt to make enterprises independent, tax-paying entities seems to have been checked for the time being. The authorities prefer to lay down individually the proportion of profits that enterprises may retain, as in this way they feel they have a better hold on them. It is feared that if enterprises were tax-paying entities they would regard the payment of taxes alone as fulfilment of their obligations towards the state and would no longer bother about state plan directives.[1]

The price freeze on certain foods and consumer goods in 1981 in order to curb inflationary tendencies contributes little towards achievement of the objectives of the reform, for by freezing prices the authorities are forgoing the indicative value of freely movable prices. The recentralisation introduced in certain manufacturing sectors also runs counter to the reform objectives. For example, enterprises in the cigarette industry have once again come under central control, for in the process of liberalising investment tobacco-growing regions built small cigarette factories and failed to keep the large modern plant in the cities supplied with sufficient tobacco. Production quotas for cigarettes and tobacco allocations are once again set centrally, with the large factories receiving priority treatment in order to exploit their cost and quality advantages. Production quotas for television manufacturers are also being set centrally again after the economic policymakers had concluded that allowing the growth of the branch to depend on decentralised production decisions was leading to undesirable oversupply. These steps towards recentralisation also affect the joint ventures with foreign companies that have been set up in this branch (paragraph 153).

113. One measure that has not yet shown whether it will help promote the development of a competitive economy is the amalgamation of enter-

1 According to recent information this assessment has to be corrected: at the beginning of 1983 the Chinese economic leadership decided to extent the profit taxation successivly to all enterprises.

prises in one and the same branch into enterprise associations or trusts.[1] In some cities or districts associations of textile factories , potteries or engineering works have already been set up. In the ship-building and lorry-building industries such associations have been established at national level. It is hoped that the advantages of large-scale production can be achieved by combining small, medium and large enterprises. Trusts procure the necessary raw materials for member enterprises and market the goods produced under their guidance, in some cases even abroad.

The amalgation of enterprises leads to an increase in the degree of concentration in the economy. The authorities see this as a way of anticipating the outcome of the competitive process of natural selection (which causes the most successful enterprises to grow and the least successful to disappear, thus leading to economic concentration). Many economic policymakers in China believe that the adverse economic and social consequences of the market economy's selection process can be avoid if enterprises co-operate with one another within an association.

The advantages of enterprise associations do not enjoy uncritical accept-ance, however. It is recognised that modern technologies and modern methods of management can be introduced more easily in large concerns than in small enterprises, but it is also pointed out that mergers easily lead to a concentration of economic power that hampers development, in other words to monopolies that are under no pressure to react flexibly and dynamically and in which it is ultimately only the bureaucrats who again set the tone. According to this view, mergers can be justified only so long as they lead to plant of optimum size from the technical and organisational points of view.

IV. The effects of the new development policy on external trade

114. A number of conclusions regarding China's foreign trade policy can be drawn from the examination of the objectives of the new development

1 See for example Renmin Ribao, 29.5.1981.

policy and the measures taken. As Chapter II contains a detailed examination of foreign trade policy itself, these conclusions are only of a
general nature based on the development priorities and the published
guidelines of foreign trade policy. They take account of the present
level of development and the problems that must be tackled in implement-
ing the procedural and organisational measures. As will be seen in
Chapter II, they correspond broadly to the guidelines for the new
foreign trade policy.

115. The next few years will see a further substantial expansion in
China's foreign trade. If the desired high rates of growth in national
income are to be achieved at the same time as a slight rise in the
consumption ratio, investments must produce the maximum growth effect.
This is to be achieved by increasing the import content of investment.
(It is assumed that capital goods from abroad generally have a higher
productivity than those produced domestically.) China will therefore
increase her imports of capital goods and at the same time try to expand
her exports in order to earn the necessary foreign exchange.

116. The large volume of foreign capital goods required will lead to a
rise in imports of capital (an increase in foreign borrowing and/or in
the volume of foreign venture capital), because domestic capital formation will be more severely limited by the expansion of consumption and
because exports to earn foreign currency can probably not be increased
quickly enough.

117. The expansion of production capacity gives rise to an immediate
need for foreign capital goods in those sectors on which development
efforts are to be concentrated under the new scheme of priorities and
in which China cannot achieve rapid results by reliance on her own
resources alone. The sectors to be developed first are light industry
and agriculture, those branches of heavy industry producing intermediate inputs for light industry and agriculture, the construction industry,
the transport sector and the communications sector. The foreign capital
goods required in these sectors covers a very wide spectrum, although
only selected examples can be mentioned here. For instance, China does

not sufficiently posess the plant for processing, conserving, packing, bottling, storing and refrigerating agricultural produce that are needed to develop an efficient food industry. By installing foreign machinery, new production capacity is to be created in the leisure electronics sector. The development of an efficient agricultural sector is to be fostered by the importation of plant to manufacture artificial fertilisers, insecticides and agricultural implements, which will be used with modern scientific methods of framing to help diversify agricultural production or counter the growing problem of soil erosion in many regions. The expansion of the energy sector is to be accelerated by importing equipment for exploration, extraction and for the processing of energy products. Finally, the government wishes to push ahead with development of the infrastructure in the widest sense - chiefly the transport and communications sectors - by importing the necessary equipment.

118. In the medium term the provision of new production capacity will not be confined to the sectors listed above. With the progresssive restructuring of the economy, not least to accomodate the production of consumer goods, it will again become necessary to expand those branches of heavy industry where cuts are being made at present. Chinese policymakers are already turning their thoughts in this direction, as may be seen in the decision that work on the construction of certain large plant that had recently been cancelled, such as the Baoshan steel mill, would begin in about three years' time. In the foreseeable future the Chinese economic leadership will display an interest in a still wider range of foreign equipment and plant. Really large projects can hardly be considered in any numbers, as finances will be stretched by the Baoshan steel complex and other building projects in the chemicals sector on which work has been postponed for a few years.

119. Food (especially grain) and consumer durables (cassette recorders, radios etc.) will be imported in order to increase the supply of consumer goods as quickly as possible. This should help satisfy the excess demand that built up because incomes were increased too quickly but the structure of manufacturing industry shifted too slowly in favour of consumer goods. Imports of high-quality consumer durables also ensure

that sufficient material incentives are offered to well-paid sections of the population. However, only very small quantities of "luxury goods" can be imported for the time being, as the ambitious growth targets require substantial imports of capital goods.

120. A larger volume of plant and equipment will also be imported to modernise existing factories. By international standards the level of productivity is very low, so that the need for modernisation is extremely great in practically all industries and regions. In view of the limited resources available, the Economic Commission intends to designate the branches and plant that will receive priority. One of the Commission's main concerns will be to improve the use of energy.

121. Powers of decision in the foreign trade field will be decentralised so that "better" import decisions will be taken. As in the domestic economy, where regional administrations and enterprises exercise delegated powers of decision over production and investment, regional authorities and in some cases enterprises or enterprise associations will have a say in import decisions. In contrast to the domestic field, there will also be a transfer of decision-making power among administrative bodies at the central government level, namely from the Ministry of Foreign Trade to ministries and other bodies that have closer ties with "production".

122. The decentralisation of import decisions is matched by comparable measures on the export side. Ministries and other central bodies, regional administrations and enterprises (or enterprise associations) will also be given some powers of decision over the marketing of their products abroad. They will be allowed to keep a share of their profits (in local or foreign currency) in order to stimulate their interest in exporting.

123. However, decentralisation will certainly not be allowed to go beyond the point where it could jeopardise the state's "foreign trade monopoly". According to current thinking that would occur if the state considered it had lost control over the flow of goods and capital between China and the rest of the world.

Chapter II

NEW DEVELOPMENTS IN FOREIGN ECONOMIC POLICY

124. The first chapter analysed the development strategy pursued since the end of the seventies, with emphasis on the domestic scene. The examination of procedural and organisational aims and measures enabled specific conclusions to be drawn with regard to external economic policy that provided general answers to the question as to the form in which China wishes to exploit foreign resources in future and in which sectors (paragraphs 114-121).

In this chapter recent developments in external economic policy will be examined in detail. First the prime policy objectives will be described; these correspond broadly to the foreign trade effects deduced from the new development policy in Chapter I. The most important measures taken so far in furtherance of these objectives will then be presented.

I.   The objectives of the new foreign economic policy

125. China's main objective in opening her borders to trade with the rest of the world is to obtain foreign goods and technology to promote her development.[1] China has great export potential on account of her large labour force and rich natural resources. By importing some capital goods from abroad, the government wishes to exploit this potential and to develop production capacity for goods that can be sold at competitive prices on the world market.

126. However, the production of export goods cannot be expanded appreciably in a short space of time, so that a shortage of foreign ex-

1   Cf. Beijing Rundschau, No. 52, 1978, p. 12.

change will prevent achievement of the country's import objectives. So that she can obtain goods she wants on world markets in spite of this, China wishes to raise foreign capital (loans and/or risk capital) on the best possible terms.

127. Measures designed to bring about "better" import and export decisions will include reform of the "foreign trade apparatus". Essentially this entails decentralisation of the powers over foreign trade previously concentrated in the hands of the Ministry of Foreign Trade and arousing self-interest by instituting profit-sharing for administrative units and enterprises involved in import and export decisions. Nevertheless, these measures will not be allowed to impair the central government's control over external trade relations.

II.   External economic policy measures

128. A series of measures have been taken to achieve the government's external economic objectives;   the main ones, which will be examined below, are

- measures to expand and diversify China's foreign trade,

- measures related to the use of foreign capital and

- institutional modifications within the external trade apparatus.

1)   The expansion and diversification of foreign trade

A   Import policy

129. In order to ensure that the composition of imports is consistent with the priorities of the new development policy, China's economic policymakers have issued guidelines that are binding on the Ministry of Foreign Trade and the other institutions and enterprises engaged in business abroad. Priority is first to be given to imports for the creation

of new production capacity in those sectors where there are currently bottlenecks (paragraphs 9, 10, 12 and 117). In addition, equipment required for the modernisation of existing plant is to be imported, with particular emphasis on energy conservation (paragraphs 43-45 and 111). Industrial inputs and consumer goods that are in particularly short supply (including very small quantities of expensive consumer goods) are also to be imported.[1] Taken together, these measures should ensure that the volume of imports grow steadily not only in nominal but also in real terms.

130. In certain sectors import requirements have already been identified more precisely. At the beginning of 1982 around 3 000 key plant[2] in the industrial and transport sectors were selected for priority modernisation (paragraph 45). About one-third of these enterprises are situated in Shanghai, Beijing and Tianjin. Their modernisation will entail the installation of domestically produced plant worth just under 2 billion Yuan and foreign equipment to the value of US-$ 270 million. In addition, in mid 1982 interested foreign parties were given a list of 130 projects[3] that they can help equip and modernise.

131. In order to enforce the new import priorities, the authorities felt it was necessary to stipulate which goods could not be imported for the time being or could be imported only on certain conditions. The main restrictions apply to plant and equipment for heavy industry except branches making an important contribution towards the development of light industry and agriculture. Imports will be permitted only in exceptional circumstances and then only subject to the provision of any necessary ancillary investment and to the availability of the energy, raw materials and transport facilities required for the plant's operation.

---

1 Cf. Guanyu woguo de duiwai jingji guanxi wenti, pp. 6 et seqq. in: Hongqi, No. 8, 1982, pp. 6 et seqq.

2 Cf. XNA, 30.3.1982.

3 The projects are listed by region and sector in: China's New Major Drive to seek Foreign Investment, in: Economic Reporter, No. 4, 1982, pp. 10 et seqq. and in: China Needs More Foreign Investment, in: Economic Reporter, No. 5, 1982, pp. 6 et seqq.

132. The importation of high-quality consumer goods has been controlled more strictly than was originally intended. When the new development policy was first launched the restrictions on imports of consumer goods were relaxed because domestic production could not meet the increase in demand caused by the wage rises. As a result, imports of consumer goods rose more quickly than expected, thus reducing the amount of foreign exchange available for imports of capital goods. Imported goods also began to compete with domestic products, which was seen as a problem mainly in those cases where domestic capacity to manufacture such goods as radios, tape recorders, wrist watches and television sets had been expanded but the goods were not selling because consumers preferred comparable imported products in spite of their higher price. Hence in mid 1982 import restrictions were introduced and a complete import ban was imposed on certain goods.[1]

133. The authorities also wish to use tariff measures to keep imports in line with the development priorities. The 1980 import duty orders reduced customs tariffs on light industrial equipment, especially for the textile industry. They also cut the duty on certain machine spares and industrial inputs imported for further processing and re-export. Lower rates of duty were also levied on primary products that are not produced in sufficient quantities domestically, such as wood and rubber. On the other hand, customs tariffs were raised on products for which adequate production capacity has now been installed (such as electricity generating plant or certain mining equipment).[2]

From this and the import restrictions described above it is clear that for the time being China has little intention of allowing domestic and foreign suppliers to compete against one another in her markets.

1 Cf. Handelsblatt, 21.7.1982.
2 Cf. China Economic News, 31.3.1980;   ZHOU Ji: Woguo haiguan dui "haiguan jinchukou shuice" jinxing tiaozheng, in: Guoji Maoyi Xiaoxi, 18.1.1982, p. 1, reprinted in: Zhongguo Renmin Daxue Shubao Ziliao She (ed.): Waimao Jingji (referred to subsequently as Waimao Jingji), No. 3, 1982, p. 102.

B   Export policy

134. As in the case of imports, guidelines have been issued to define
the areas in which ministries, regional administrations and enterprises
are to concentrate their export and production efforts. As labour costs
are low by international standards, exports are to consist of labour-
intensive products, primarily textiles and handicrafts.[1] The export
prospects of other manufactured products such as machinery or electrical goods are still regarded as slim, but larger quantities of these
goods are to be sold abroad in order to increase the proportion of
high-value products in total exports[2] (particularly as these industries
have spare capacity during the restructuring). At present the potential
buyers of such products are other developing countries, but in the
medium term China wants to break into the markets of industrialised
countries as well. (A start has already been made by means of co-operation in the engineering sector.) Exports of agricultural produce are also
to be stepped up, although serious bottlenecks in processing and packing as well as in production are still an impediment. Once these problems
have been resolved the produce can be sold not only in Hong Kong but
also in more distant markets.

135. Finally, the government wants to develop China's raw materials for
export. The country has rich deposits of coal, mineral oil, iron ore and
non-ferrous metals. According to Chinese sources proven coal reserves
amount to 640 billion tonnes, about two-thirds of which are located in
the north of the country. Many of the deposits are such that they can
be mined cheaply and the grades available are in high international
demand. However, production capacity can cover only domestic requirements. Only about 1 per cent of the annual production of about 600
million tonnes of raw coal has been exported up to now, and production
has been stagnating for the last few years. Heavy investment in extrac-

1 Cf. JI Chongwei: Yingyong bijiao chengbenlun zhidao woguo duiwai
   maoyi, zai guoji maoyi zhong qude jiao hao de jingji xiaoguo, in:
   Waimao Jiaoxue yu Yanjiu, No. 3, 1981, pp. 1-13, reprinted in: Waimao
   Jingji, No. 3, 1982, pp. 84 et seqq.

2 Cf. WANG Yihe: Woguo chukou maoyi pouxi - zou guangda chukou de
   xin luzi, in: Shehui Kexue, No. 6, 1981, pp. 12-19, reprinted in:
   Waimao Jingji, No. 2, 1982, pp. 90 et seqq.

tion equipment, dressing plant and above all the transport system will be needed to increase production. If this course is adopted, exports of coal cannot be expected to increase until the second half of the eighties at the earliest.

Foreign sources put a figure of about 2.7 billion tonnes on proven oil reserves (by way of comparison, Saudi Arabia's proven reserves total about 22 billion tonnes). The geophysical structures give cause to believe that potential oil reserves are much higher; in Chinese publications they are estimated at anything up to 60 billion tonnes,[1] but the picture is unclear as prospecting has scarcely begun. Oil production, which like coal production has stagnated since 1978, is running at just over 100 million tonnes, of which about 15 per cent is exported to Japan, Hong Kong, Thailand, the Philippines and Rumania.[2] The existing wells are nearing depletion, so that decline in oil production is feared unless new deposits can be exploited in time, particularly off shore.[3] Over the medium term, however, the prospects for oil production look good; foreign firms are prepared to play a major part in exploration and extraction. One estimate, which is regarded as optimistic, puts oil production in 1990 at 200 million tonnes and exports at 50 million tonnes.[4]

Besides energy-bearing raw materials, China has extensive deposits of metalliferous ores and rare earths. By her own assessment, China heads the world tables with its deposits of tungsten, tin, antimony, zinc, titanium, tantalum and rare earths. Reserves of lead, nickel, mercury, molybdenum, niobium, copper and bauxite are among the largest in the world.[5] China is already a major exporter of certain metals such as tungsten, antimony, tin and zinc, but she cannot cover even domestic demand for other ores because of a lack of production capacity. Even

1 Cf. SAI Feng: Woguo shiyou ziyuan de qianjing yu pucha kantan renwu, in: Renmin Ribao, 16.4.1982.

2 Cf. China Newsletter, No. 37, March-April 1982, p. 24.

3 Cfl. WIESEGART, Kurt: Oil from Chinese Deposits, in: Intereconomics, November-December 1980, pp. 308 et seqq.

4 Cf. The Journal of Commerce, October 1982.

5 Cf. Beijing Rundschau, No. 10, 1982, p. 7.

iron ore must still be imported. Considerable investment in exploration, dressing and processing ist still needed if the available deposits are to cover domestic requirements and help increase the volume of exports. Moreover, development of the transport sector is a prerequisite for exploitation of the deposits.

136. A series of concrete measures have already been taken to expand exports. There have long been enterprises manufacturing industrial products or processing agricultural produce exclusively for export. Some of these are situated in special export goods production centres.[1] The number of such enterprises has been increased and their production capacity expanded. There are now export enterprises in 114 export goods production centres and almost 100 further individual factories producing specially for overseas markets. In 1981 they produced export goods worth 9.25 billion Yuan, which represented more than 20 per cent of the goods exported that year.[2]

137. The Yuan has been devalued de facto to offer greater incentive to the government bodies, companies and enterprises that now receive a share of their export earnings (see section 3 below). Export earnings are no longer converted at the rate of about Yuan 1.5 to the US dollar (which corresponds to the tourist rate) but at about Yuan 2.8, so that export business has become more "profitable". (The devalued Yuan rate is also applied to importing enterprises, so that imports become more expensive and are thus curbed.)[3]

138. Since the decentralisation of the foreign trade system foreign trade flows have not been under the direct guidance and control of a single body, namely the Ministry of Foreign Trade, so that customs measures

1 The first export goods production centres were established in 1960. Cf. WANG Shouchun, LI Kanghua: Fazhan chukou shangpin shengchan jidi, in: HU Qiaomu (ed.): Zhongguo Baike Nianjian, Shanghai 1981, p. 213; also: Ba chukou shangpin jidi jianshe hao, in: Renmin Ribao, 19.6.1979.

2 Cf. XNA, 6.6.1982.

3 Cf. WIESEGART, Kurt: Für Importunternehmen hängt der Korb höher, in: Handelsblatt, 8.2.1982.

have been taken to enforce certain priorities in the composition of exports. Since June 1982 more than 30 items (such as coal, tungsten, antimony, rice and sugar) have been subject to export duties ranging vom 10 per cent to 60 per cent. These have been imposed to prevent goods with domestic prices that are low in relation to those on the world market (coal, tungsten, antimony, etc.) from being exported too cheaply and in excessively large quantities, thus causing bottlenecks at home and ultimately harming the economy. In addition, a system of export licensing has been introduced for certain goods; it applies to almost 50 items in 11 product groups, on some of which export duties are also levied. These include mineral oil and coal.[1]

139. In order to break down trade barriers abroad and generally to create favourable conditions for the export of Chinese goods, China is making great efforts to conclude trade agreements. China was one of the first socialist countries to recognise the EEC and signed a trade agreement with the Community so that she could enjoy trade concessions.

C   The development of imports and exports

140.   Since 1978 both imports and exports have recorded extremely high rates of growth (see Tables 2 and 3). According to Chinese data imports (expressed in Yuan) increased by just under 100 per cent between 1978 and 1981 while exports rose by as much as 120 per cent. Somewhat different growth rates are obtained, however, if one takes the foreign trade statistics of China's trading partners. On this basis Chinese exports (in US dollars) still showed a rise of 120 per cent over the same period but imports rose by almost 80 per cent.

141. On the import side certain products show marked changes that are partly due to the new import priorities. For example, iron and steel imports declined from US-$ 3.4 billion in 1979 to US-$ 1.7 billion in

1 Cf. Nachrichten für Außenhandel, No. 106, 4.6.1982, and No. 113, 16. 6.1982.

Table 2   FOREIGN TRADE IN YUAN FROM 1978 TO 1981

	Exports (bn Yuan)	Imports (bn Yuan)
1978	16 760	18 740
1979	21 200	24 300
1980	27 200	29 100
1981	36 760	36 770

Sources: Communiqués 1978, 1979, 1980 und 1981.

Table 3   FOREIGN TRADE IN US DOLLARS FROM 1978 TO 1981

	Exports (f.o.b.) (bn US $)	Imports (c.i.f.) (bn US $)
1978	10 177	11 224
1979	13 736	15 731
1980	19 342	20 908
1981	22 377	20 029

Source: China: International Trade, Fourth Quarter, 1981, CIA, June 1982.

1981. Over the same period imports of textile fibres rose from US-$ 1.1 to 2 billion and those of textile yarn from US-$ 0.3 to 1.6 billion. Grain imports increased from US-$ 1.3 to 2.2 billion. In 1981 the composition of overall imports was as follows: foodstuffs c. 15 per cent, raw materials c. 15 per cent, chemicals c. 10 per cent, semi-finished goods c. 25 per cent and plant and machinery just under 30 per cent.[1]

1 Cf. China: International Trade, Fourth Quarter 1981, CIA, June 1982.

142. Exports of certain goods also show notable changes that may be seen partly as an early result of applying the new export priorities. Exports of petroleum and chemicals rose from US-$ 2.2 billion in 1979 to US-$ 4.5 billion in 1981. Over the same period export of textiles rose from US-$ 3.3 to 5.4 billion and those of machinery and equipment increased from about US-$ 0.5 billion to almost US-$ 1 billion. Receipts from merchandise exports in 1981 break down as follows according to product group: foodstuffs c.15 per cent, raw materials c. 10 per cent, fossil fuels over 20 per cent and semi-finished and finished goods about 50 per cent.[1]

143. According to the foreign trade statistics of China's western trading partners, China recorded a foreign currency surplus of more than US-$ 2 billion on trade transactions in 1981, the first surplus for many years. The trade deficit had amounted to about US-$ 1 billion in 1978, US-$ 2 billion in 1979 and US-$ 1.5 billion in 1980.[1]

According to Chinese data, by contrast, the trade balance showed a deficit in 1981, albeit only US-$ 0.1 billion; according to these data the trade deficit had amounted to about 2 billion Yuan in 1978, about 3 billion Yuan in 1979 and about 2 billion Yuan in 1980.[2] (The large surplus on trade account in 1981 shown by the western statistics would make it difficult for China to obtain loans from international organisations.)

The 1981 foreign trade result, which was very good for China, was achieved because that year practically no complete plant were imported owing to the cancellation of a number of large projects and because imports for the modernisation of existing plant were getting off to a slow start. If China wants to achieve her development objectives, however, imports of plant and equipment will have to rise appreciably. The scope for expanding merchandise exports, by contrast, is still relatively limited at present.

1 Cf. China: International Trade, Fourth Quarter 1981, CIA, June 1982.
2 Cf. Communiqués 1978, 1979, 1980 and 1981.

Apart from exports of goods, China wants to meet her substantial foreign currency requirement by earning additional sums from other activities that generate foreign exchange. China has taken positive steps to promote tourism by building additional hotel accomodation, partly with foreign participation. (Between 1978 and 1981 China was already able to increase her foreign currency earnings from tourism from US-$ 0.37 to 0.81 billion; the World Bank estimates that annual growth rates in the region of 20 per cent might be achieved in this sector until 1985.) The government is also seeking to earn additional foreign exchange in the transport and insurance sectors. (In 1980 the net revenue from these activities came to about US-$ 0.8 billion). To this end the merchant fleet is being increased and the insurance sector expanded. "Exports of labour" are to have a more positive effect on the foreign exchange account than hitherto; accordingly, construction and engineering companies have been founded to undertake building projects abroad. By the end of 1981 17 000 Chinese workers were already engaged on projects abroad;[1] China hopes to raise this figure to 50 000 in the near future.[2] Finally, receipts of foreign exchange are to be increased by offering special interest terms and other incentives on sums transferred back to China by Chinese living abroad. (Transfers by ex-patriate Chinese came to about US-$ 0.7 billion in 1980.)

Even if merchandise exports and invisible earnings show satisfactory growth, in all probability foreign currency earnings will be insufficient to finance the country's import requirements in the years to come, assuming that the economic policymakers hold to their development course.

Hence the need for foreign capital will probably increase in the next few years.

---

1 Cf. China Daily, 30.3.1982. By mid 1982 the number had already risen to 25 000. Most of the workers are engaged on construction projects in countries in the Middle East. Cf. China Daily, 28.7.1982.

2 Cf. The Financial Times, 24.8.1981.

2) The use of foreign capital

144. The various measures that China's economic policymakers have taken to attract foreign capital will be examined below. China has negotiated credit lines with foreign governments and banks. She has joined international organisations and gained access to loans in this way. In addition, she has raised equity capital on the basis of joint ventures and other forms of co-operation and concluded compensation trade and commission processing deals. Special forms of co-operation with foreign firms have been applied in the development of energy resources. Finally, special economic zones have been created in order to concentrate the various forms of co-operation geographically and thus to exploit them more fully.

A Foreign loans

145. At the end of the seventies China began to seek credit comittments from foreign governments, banks and international organisations in order to establish a substantial line of credit and at the same time build up a wide circle of potential lenders so that she could choose among various sources of credit and avoid becoming dependent upon individual lenders. As there was great willingness in the West to grant China loans to finance her imports, the total of opened credit lines quickly grew. By the end of 1981 credit commitments reportedly totalled about US-$ 30 billion.[1]

146. The bulk of the loans were granted by governments under export credit agreements. According to official figures released by the Bank of China, agreements involving a total of US-$ 12.7 billion had been concluded with more that ten countries by the end of 1981. Japanese estimates put the total as high as US-$ 17 billion. The majority of the credit offered have a life of between 5 and 10 years; interest rates are fixed, most falling between 7.25 per cent and 7.5 per cent[2] - at this level some may need to be subsidised by the lending country.

1 Cf. YAMADA, Yasuhiro: China's Foreign financial Position, in: China Newsletter, No. 35, November-December 1981, pp. 2 et seqq.

2 Ibid., p. 3.

Commercial banks have also opened credti lines for China totalling about US-\$ 10 billion, according to Japanese estimates. This sum includes a short-term bridging loan (60 days) amounting to about US-\$ 6 billion that was extended by a Japanese banking consortium in mid 1979 to cover any liquidity shortages arising from imports of large plant from Japan. The remaining credits mostly have a life of up to five years; the interest rates offered generally lie 0.5 per cent above LIBOR.[1]

Finally, the governments of certain countries (Japan, Belgium) and international organisations (the international Monetary Fund, the World Bank, UN agencies) have promised China loans on particularly favour-able terms. The amount involved totalled about US-\$ 4 billion at the end of 1981. This includes yen-dominated loans for energy projects worth about US-\$ 2 billion offered by the Japanese Ex-Im Bank. These loans are very long and the interest rates very low in some cases only handling fees are charged.[2]

147. Until the end of 1981 only US-\$ 45 billion on the credit lines had been utilised. The bulk of the funds had been drawn from the IMF and the World Bank (US-\$ 1.6 billion) and from the development funds provides by Japan (US-\$ 1.5 billion according to Chinese data). Very little has yet been borrowed under the loan commitments of the various governments and commercial banks, as China is reluctant to pay the relatively high interest rates and has been able to cover her require-ment for foreign capital so far by raising equity capital and by means of other forms of economic co-operation.

B   Equity capital and co-operation

148. Many of the forms of co-operation with western companies that were developed in the late seventies are new to China. They were modelled on similar arrangements and experiences in other countries (South Korea, Taiwan, Singapore, the countries of Eastern Europe) but

1 Cf. YAMADA, Yasuhiro: loc. cit., p. 4.
2 Ibid., pp. 5 et seqq.; see also Shijie Jingji Daobao, 5.4.1982.

ready-made concepts were not applied. The Chinese first wanted to gain experience with a small number of "pilot schemes" and then lay down the organisational and legal framework accordingly, it is hoped that certain less desirable consequences of employing foreign equity capital, such as foreign influences on production and trade, can be held within acceptable bounds by means of statutory requirements, customs regulations and the like while at the same time ensuring that such business deals remain attractive to foreign partners.

149. China is now using practically the full spectrum of the customary forms of international co-operation. The various co-operation agreement take such diverse forms that they cannot always be classified clearly under a specific form of co-operation. The classification is relatively easy in the case of agreements based on the Joint Venture Law passed in 1979; these are so-called equity joint ventures, where the foreign investors play a part in management and where profits of losses are shared in proportion to the capital contribution of the two partners. There are also contractual joint ventures, to which the Joint Venture Law does not apply. In this case the contracting parties have greater freedom to arrange the relationship between them; for example, the management may be appointed solely by the foreign partner, but it is also possible for the foreign party to play absolutely no part in the running of the enterprise. It can be agreed that the foreign partner will receive no part of the profits but will be repaid his investment in the form of finished products. In this case contracual joint ventures would show some resemblance to compensation trade projects, which are also concluded in China. Commission processing deals also occur, whereby Chinese enterprises obtain inputs from foreign firms, turn them into semi-finished of finished products and deliver them to their foreign principal. These deals often present some characteristics of compensation trade as well, such as where commission processing agreements stipulate the provision of manufacturing machinery that will be paid for in finished goods.[1] The main feature of these various forms of co-operation will be examined below. Forms of co-operation used in the

1 With regard to the problems of classifying individual forms of co-operation in East-West trade see Bolz, Klaus, and PLÖTZ, Peter: Erfahrungen aus der Ost-West-Kooperation, Hamburg 1974, pp. 22 et seqq.

energy sector and the special economic zones will then be treated separately in view of the specific questions they raise.

a)   Equity joint ventures

150. The closest co-operation generally occurs in equity joint ventures, the form of which is governed by the Law of Joint Ventures Using Chinese and Foreign Investment. This stipulates that foreign partnerships, companies of other entities must take a capital interest of at least 25 per cent in an enterprise; it sets no upper limit on their capital holdings. Equity joint ventures are to be managed jointly by the contracting parties, but the chairman of the board of directors must be appointed by the Chinese side. In principle their products are to be exported, but exceptions to this rule are possible and may be stipulated in the individual contract.[1]

The Law on Joint Ventures merely provides a framework in which many points need to be expanded and agreed case by case. Amending legislation and regulations have since been introduced, such as the regulations on exchange control, the registration and administration of joint ventures and the Income Tax Law Concerning Foreign Enterprises. However, other important laws and regulations are still lacking; for example, there is still no law to protect licences and patents, although it is envisaged that a patent law will be worked out with the assistance of the European Patent Office.[2]

151. Close collaboration between Chinese and western partners over long periods raises the possibility of various kinds of conflict owing to the different interests of the two partners. For example, the foreign partner is interested in opening the Chinese market to his products and in earning profits, while the Chinese partner, on the other hand is often required to run the enterprise in accordance with the economic

1 Cf. The Law of the People's Republic of China on Joint Ventures using
   Chinese and Foreign Investment, Beijing Rundschau, No. 29, 1979, pp.
   25 et seqq.
2 Cf. Handelsblatt, 21.5.1982.

objectives of higher administrative authorities. Conflict can also easily stem from the different social and cultural allegiances of the two partners. Western partners, which must produce results for their parent companies, are generally more interested in swift decisions and if necessary are more prepared to bring conflicts into the open than are their Chinese partners, who are inclined to postpone difficult decisions for the sake of maintaining consensus.[1]

China is prepared to grant special conditions for foreign investors in order to increase the attraction of equity joint ventures in China for western partners. In certain circumstances reductions in taxes such as corporation tax are possible and if certain conditions are fulfilled raw materials, intermediate inputs and equipment can be imported duty free. As a rule equity joint ventures enjoy priority over purely Chinese enterprises in the supply of raw materials, energy and finance. They are also largely free to engage and dismiss labour.

152. By the end of 1981 a total of forty equity joint ventures had been approved by the competent authorities and almost thirty of these had already begun operations. Chinese sources give the foreign capital investment as US-$ 87.5 million[2] and the Chinese contributions as US-$ 100 million. The foreign investment varies between US-$ 0.1 and 36 million.[3] In thirtyfive of the forty enterprises the total investment is less than US-$ 10 million.[4] Foreign partners have generally contributed modern equipment and technical know how in the form of licences and patents, while the Chinese have usually provided factory buildings and land usage rights. Fifteen of the forty joint ventures are in light industry (including the textile industry), nine are in the

1 Cf. KLENNER, Wolfgang, and WIESEGART, Kurt: Joint Ventures in the PR China, in: Intereconomics, March-April 1980, pp. 89 et seqq.

2 Cf. XNA, 8.6.1982. This figure of US-$ 87.5 million presumably relates only to capital that has already been transferred. No precise information is available on the total amount of foreign capital to be invested.

3 Cf. What's Happening in Chinese Joint Ventures, in: JETRO China Newsletter, No. 36, 1982, pp. 22 et seqq.

4 Cf. JI Chongwei: Chinas Kapazität zur Aufnahme ausländischer Investitionen, in: Beijing Rundschau, No. 17, 1982, pp. 20 et seqq.

mechanical and electrical engineering sectors and three in the food-processing industry. Eight enterprises were set up in the services sector, primarily the hotel trade. Finally, three animal breeding stations, a pharmaceutical factory and a leasing company are being run as equity joint ventures. More than half the partners come from Hong Kong (16 companies). Other enterprises involve firms from Japan (4), the Philippines (3), the USA (2), the Federal Republic of Germany, Switzerland, the United Kingdom, France, Singapore and Canada (one firm each).[1]

153. Most of the equity joint ventures are still in the start-up phase. The profits of only two enterprises have been reported; these are Beijing Air Catering and China Schindler Elevator Shanghai.[2] In most of the other enterprises the partners are no doubt still at the stage of clarifying matters such as their differing interests, organisation of the enterprise and so forth. During the start-up phase of such co-operation schemes it is often discovered that some points settled in the contract cannot be realised in the manner intended and that no provision has been made for other points. This can inevitably lead to disappointment on both sides. The experiences of Fujian Hitachi Television provide an example of how easily the expectations of foreign partners can prove to be exaggerated. This enterprise had increased its production capacity to 300 000 television sets a year as foreseen in the contract. In the meanwhile, it was instructed "from above" to produce no more than 230 000 sets a year and what is more, it was forbidden to sell its products in any Chinese provinces except the province of Fujian.[3]

1   Cf.   JI Chongwei, loc. cit.
2   The   profits of these two enterprises could be described as extremely high in relation to the capital employed. In its first year of operation Beijing Air Catering returned a profit of 550 000 Yuan (about US-$ 320 000) on capital of about US $ 3.9 million (the Hong Kong partner's share amounted to 49 per cent). In its first year of trading China Schindlers Elevator recorded profits equal to almost 25 per cent of the capital, i.e. US-$ 3.6 million (the Swiss firm Schindler Holding AG and its Hong Kong subsidiary hold 25 per cent of the capital of US-$ 16 million). Cf. What's Happening ..., op. cit., pp. 18 et seqq.
3   Cf.   The Japan Economic Journal, 22.6.1982.

154. China is interested in seeing further equity joint ventures established and therefore intends to speed up the process of examination and approval. Those who wish to push ahead with the economic reforms hope that joint ventures will have a knock-on effect. The attitude of foreign investigations into joint ventures in China will depend on the business results of those that have already been established. The perceived climate for co-operation and the medium-term prospects of breaking into the Chinese market will also play a not unimportant role.

b)   Contractual joint ventures

155. China's keen interest in joint enterprises of every kind can be judged from the fact that the provisions of the Law on Joint Ventures are not binding on all forms of co-operation involving foreign capital. Foreign and Chinese partners are at perfect liberty to conclude individual contracts that diverge from the provisions of the law on Joint Ventures with regard to the level of their capital participation, their right to a voice in management and the arrangements for profitsharing. Contracts drawn hitherto have generally stipulated that, unless it is extended contractually, the relationship will terminate when the foreign capital contributions have been repaid in foreign currency or in the form of finished goods (including an adequate provision for profit).

156. The possibility of arranging the conditions of joint production to suit the project aroused great interest abroad. By the end of 1981 390 such contracts relating to foreign investment totalling US-$ 1.8 billion had been concluded.[1] The scale of foreign capital contributions ranges from a few hundred thousand US dollars to US-$ 50 million. Most of the projects are in light industry, tourism, residential construction and services and are located predominately in the provinces of Guangdong and Fujian. The majority of the foreign partners come from Hong Kong and Japan.[2]

1   Cf.   XNA, 8.6.1982.
2   Cf.   China Trade Report, May 1982.

157. As may be gauged from the intention of the Chinese policymakers to give contractual joint ventures similar priority to that enjoyed by equity joint ventures,[1] such as in the supply of production factors, there is great interest in establishing further enterprises of this nature.

For Westerners contractual joint ventures are attractive on account of the possibility of drawing contracts individually and thereby ensuring that, for example, their capital contributions will be repaid with an adequate prodit.

c)   Compensation Trade

158. As in the case of contractual joint ventures, the parties to compensation trade[2] deals can draw contracts more of less as they wish. By the end of 1981 590 compensation agreements had been concluded under which plant and equipment to the value of about US-$ 460 million was imported.[3] Most provide for settlement to be completed in the form of shipments of goods two or three years after supply of the plant or machinery, although for a very small number of large projects the period is set at seven to eight years. Up to now imports under compensation trade have been used mainly in the expansion and modernisation of light industry, in particular the textile industry. A large number of the projects are situated in Guangdong province. Partner firms come mostly from Hong Kong and Macao, and further third are Japanese companies.

---

1   The government intends to grant them special rights in the field of production planning, procurement of materials and finance and with regard to the engagement and dismissal of workers. Cf. XNA, 6.6.1982.

2   The modes of business usually applied in trade with countries low in foreign currency reserves are barter trade, product buyback, and product sharing. The more general term for these modes of trade is "compensation trade". This is especially prevalent in trade with East European countries, where imports of machinery and equipment are paid for in part or whole with goods produced by this machinery and equipment.

3   Cf. XNA, 6.6.1982.

159. China would like to make greater use of compensation trade because theiy allow plant and equipment to be imported in exchange for precise quantities of goods that can be planned into production schedules and remove the need to generate foreign exchange in advance by selling suitable products on the world market. Local authorities and even Chinese enterprises themselves are to be given guidance and information about product prices. price variations on the world market and exchange rate fluctuations to enable them to obtain better contract terms in future.[1] Western trading partners may not welcome the restriction on the free exchange of goods that compensation trade entails, but the growth of such business in trade with eastern European countries has shown that they are well able to look after their interests where this form of trade is concerned.

d)   Commission processing deals

160. By the end of 1981 nearly 10 000 commission processing agreements had been signed with foreign counterparts. In the first eight months of 1981 China earned US-$ 110 million from such contracts, twice as much as in the same period of the preceding year.[2] The bulk of the agreements related to goods produced by light industry. The enterprises involved were situated mostly in Guangdong and Shanghai, while the majority of the commissioning firms came from Hong Kong and Macao.

---

1 Chinese publications carry complaints that in many cases decentralisation has led inexperienced Chinese negotiators to sign contracts with foreign companies that are disadvantageous to the Chinese sinde. This is said to be particularly common in the case of compensation trade, the complexities of which are often not recognised by the Chinese contracting parties for lack of experience. Cf. WANG Shanqing: Buchang maoyi zhong zhide zhongshe de wenti, in: Shijie Jingji Daobao, 29.3.1982. Similar problems are aldo detected with co-operation projects abroad. Cf. GUO Hanbin: Woguo zai guowai kaiban hezi jingying qiye jige wenti, in: Jingji Cankao, 15.2.1982, p. 4, reprinted in: Waimao Jingji No. 3 1982, p. 74.

2 Cf. XNA, 2.10.1981.

e)   Co-operation in the energy sector

161. China also gives foreign enterprises a part to play in the development and exploitation of her vast energy resources. The Chinese maintain that the large capital requirement and long-term nature of the
projects and the high commercial risk associated with the work of exploration and development call for special forms of co-operation. Under
the agreements concluded so far in the energy sector the foreign partners are to provide their capital investment in the shape of exploration
and development work and are to receive a share of the energy products extracted, but only if the project is successful.

The participation of foreign firms in the exploitation of China's natural
resources was long a subject of heated debate. It was feared that
China's independence could be seriously curtailed if foreign companies
were given access to her mineral wealth. However, the authorities
eventually came down in favour of co-operation with foreign firms in the
energy sector too, as the removal of bottlenecks in this field had been
one of the most pressing problems for many years and as the chances
of China developing her energy resources solely by her own means were
regarded as slim.

162. Co-operation agreements have been concluded so far with French
and Japanese oil companies for the development of hydrocarbon deposits.
The contracts provide for the Chinese and foreign parties to contribute
stated proportions of the capital required for exploration, development
and extraction of deposits and for part of the earnings after taxation to
be used for further development and part to be distributed among the
contracting parties.[1] The agreements provide for co-operation in the
Gulf of Bohai and the Gulf of Beibu. By mid 1982 the French and
Japanese firms had already carried out investment worth US-$ 460
million.[2]

---

1   Cf.   WIESEGART, Kurt: Oil from Chinese Deposits,   loc. cit., pp. 311
    et seqq.
2   Cf.   XNA, 8.6.1982.

Similar agreements will probably be signed with these and other oil companies for the development of the offshore fields. At the beginning of 1982 tenders were invited for exploratory drilling in further offshore areas. Foreign oil companies are keenly interested in such agreements in spite of the high risk, as can be seen from the fact that for several years 48 oil companies have been carrying out geophysical surveys in offshore regions at their own expense so that they would be in a fa- vourable position to apply for drilling rights and to negotiate contract terms.[1]   The Chinese policymakers now propose to use foreign capital in the exploration for onshore deposits as well.

163. The Chinese are also negotiating with foreign firms over the devel- opment of coal deposits. The largest such projects include the open-cast coal mine at Pingshuo in Shanxi province (negotiations with an American firm are already well advanced)[2]   and the Liupanshui coalfield in Gui- zhou province, in which both American and Belgian firms have shown an interest.[3] West German, American, Japanese, British, French and Belgian companies are interested in developing further coal reserves in Shanxi province and in the coalfields of Huainan-Huaibei, Kailuan and elsewhere. The Chinese leadership wants foreign investors to help develop not only the mines but also the necessary infrastructure. Repayment would take the form of exports of energy products as far as possible.

f)   The establishment of special economic zones

164. In certain areas of the country, the so-called special economic zones, foreign investors are offered more attractive incentives than

1 Cf. Beijing Rundschau, No. 13, 1982, p. 11.

2 Investment on development of the Pingshuo deposit is put at US-$
   500-600 million by Chinese sources. The US capital investment under
   negotiation amounts to about US-$ 230 million for the first stage of
   the project. Cf. China Daily, 26.3.1982.

3 The Chinese estimate that development of the Liupanshui coalfield and
   the necessary infrastructure will require investment of several
   billion US dollars. Cf. Nachrichten für Außenhandel, No. 105,
   3.6.1982

elsewhere in China, including favourable customs regulations, low rates of corporation tax, low land rents and liberalised administrative procedures. These concessions are designed to arouse the interest of foreign companies in developing the regions by participating in equity or contractual joint ventures of engaging in compensation or commission processing deals. China is aiming not merely to win foreign capital without increasing her indebtedness; in the medium term at least she hopes to increase her foreign currency receipts by this means, because plant in special economic zones are to produce mainly for export. Moreover, it is hoped that the modern technology and methods of organisation associated with imports of capital will not only speed up the economic development of the special economic zones themselves but will also stimulate that of the country as a whole over the medium term via the knock-on effects they should generate. [1]

165. The areas of Shenzhen, Zhuhai, Shantou and the island of Hainan in Guangdong province and the island of Xiamen in Fujian province have already been designated special economic zones. Foreign investment will mainly be directed towards developing these regions as industrial centres. Tourist resorts are also to be built on Hainan and Xiamen. It is also intended that raw materials and agriculture will be developed on Hainan. [2]

A crucial factor in the choice of Guangdong and Fujian as the locations for special economic zones was their good transport connections to Hong Kong and to overseas markets. Both provinces also have ethnic ties with Hong Kong, the countries of South-east Asia and other Chinese communities abroad. It is believed that because of their family ties the businessmen among the ex-patriate Chinese will be prepared to invest in their home provinces if they are offered attractive terms.

1 Cf. FAN Zhuofen: Lun jingji tequ de xingshi, in: Jingji Yanjiu, No. 6, 1981, pp. 54 et seqq.
2 Cf. LOONG, Pauline: Special Zones, Special Rules, in: Far Eastern Economic Review, No. 38, 12.9.1980; China Economic News, 1.9.1982; Ta Kung Pao, 20-26.8.1981; China Trade Report, August 1981; Blick durch die Wirtschaft, 31.12.1981.

166. The investment conditions laid down in the government orders differ from one special economic zone to another. For example, land rents and wage rates are much lower in Xiamen than in Shenzhen, but the latter offers considerable geographical advantages owing to its position directly north of Hong Kong. [1]

167. At present the most developed of the special economic zones is Shenzhen. By the end of 1981 contracts for foreign investment totalling about US-$ 1.3 billion had been signed and plant and equipment worth US-$ 200 million had been imported for joint ventures and under compensation trade and commission processing deals. [2]   Most of the foreign partners came from Hong Kong and Macao, but investment has also been undertaken by western firms from Switzerland (engineering), Denmark (construction of containers) and Australia (quarrying). [3]

168. The Chinese consider their experience with special economic zones to have been positive in the main. Nonetheless, a number of problems have to be tackled. Besides black marketeering and foreign currency smuggling, tension has developed between the population of the special economic zones, where good performance is well rewarded, and that in neighbouring regions. Over the medium term China sees the danger that the special economic zones will become too dependent on cyclicyl changes in world markets. [4]   Nonetheless, China's economic policymakers consider that the advantages far outweigh the disadvantages. They have therefore decided on the further development of the special economic zones. The projects carried out hitherto have mainly been of small or medium size; now China also wants to harness foreign capital for the development of an efficient infrastructure in the widest sense. Advocates of special economic zones have even proposed that the entire provinces of

1   Cf.   China Trade Report, August 1981.

2   Cf.   China Daily, 27.2.1982 and 18.3.1982.

3   Cf.   Beijing Rundschau, No. 15, 1982, p. 5.

4   Cf.   DONG Qing: Feilüpin de chukou jiagongqu, in: Gongye Jingji Guanli Congkan, No. 4, 1981, pp. 68-70, reprinted in: Zhongguo Renmin Daxue Shubao Ziliao She (ed.): Gongye Jingji, Series 3, No. 12, 1981, p. 84.

Guangdong and Fujian be designated as SEZs on the grounds that it would then be easier to attract the foreign capital needed for their development. (The current five-year plan for Fujian province provides for investment totalling 5.5 billion Yuan; foreign capital requirements have been set at 1.4 billion Yuan, about US-$ 850 million.)[1]

It is still too early to predict the development prospects of the special economic zones. Whatever their future, the interest of foreign partners in capital investment and co-operation in the special economic zones is as keen as ever, particularly in regard to investments that are amortised in a relatively short space of time.

3) Institutional reforms

169. The Chinese leadership regards the structures and functions of the foreign trade apparatus built up in the fifties as the main obstacle to "better" imports, to the development of forms of finance that better suit China's import requirements and to larger and more profitable exports. Previously it was held that the domestic and external sectors of the economy had to be separate from one another in accordance with the Leninist concept of protecting the socialist economic order from foreign influences. Producers and consumers within the country could come into contact with overseas markets only via the Ministry of Foreign Trade and its foreign trade corporations specialising in particular categories of imports and exports. In this way Chinese enterprises were completely isolated from the world market.

All imports had to be approved by the central authorities and incorporated into the foreign trade plan. Time-consuming bureaucratic formalities had to be completed even if a small volume of goods was to be

---

1 Cf. STEPANEK, James B.: China's SEZ's, in: The China Business Review, March-April 1982, pp. 38 et seqq.

imported. Hence short-term opportunities on the world market were mostly missed.[1]

Exports were also subject to cumbersome procedures that curbed initiative. As a rule, exporters had to meet the requirements of several higher bodies: the relevant industrial ministries or industry bureaux that set production targets, the labour offices that laid down wage rates and employment conditions and the Ministry of Foreign Trade or certain foreign trade corporations that imposed quite specific requirements with regard to consignment quantities, quality and supply dates. The enterprises themselves were left with virtually no freedom to take their own decisions or actions. Their "subordination to several step-mothers",[2] as it is termed by Chinese critics, not only suppressed all initiative on the part of the enterprises but also condemned them to inertia, so that the flexible adjustment of export production to changes in demand on the world market was permanently blocked.

170. The reform of the foreign trade machinery that was initiated in the late seventies is based primarily on the principles outlined below. End users should be closely involved in decisions to import either goods or capital. For this purpose they are to be placed in a position to assess what the world market has to offer. Where possible, export decisions are to be taken by those concerned with production of the goods in question; they should at least have a say in decision-making. This presupposes that they can obtain information on world market demand. They should also receive a share of their export earnings.

In China users and "units" concerned with the production of export goods do not necessarily or exclusively imply enterprises or enterprise associations. It also means the ministries (at central government level), bureaux (at a regional level) and other bodies that are directly concern-

---

1 Cf. XUE Muqiao: Zhongguo shehuizhuyi jingji wenti yanjiu, loc.cit., p. 213.

2 See for example PAN Enqi: Ban hao chukou zhuanchang geng hao de wei jingji tiaozheng fuwu, in: Caimao jingji, No. 3, 1981, pp. 26 et seqq., reprinted in: Waimao Jingji, No. 9, 1981, p. 81.

ed with the management of production and, where applicable, trade. These bodies or special companies to be set up by them for overseas business purposes are no longer to take decisions concerning production, imports and exports on the basis of "administrative" criteria. Instead they are to behave as economic entities with their own profit and loss accounts and hence to be just as interested as enterprises in reaching economically sound import and export decisions. The Ministry of Foreign Trade will then concentrate mainly on administrative tasks and on the central co-ordination and supervision of flows of trade and payments (the external trade monopoly).

It is not yet clear how these principles are to be realised in detail. Much will depend on the progress of the domestic economic reform programme, which will in any case determine the course to be followed in the external sector.

171. The first steps towards putting the principles into effect have already been taken, however. At the central government level the Ministry of Foreign Trade has been reorganised and a considerable part of its previous business responsibilities have been transferred to other central agencies, the regions and, in some instances, to enterprises. The industrial ministries, in other words the ministries that oversee production in industrial enterprises under their control, have been given certain powers for planning, directing and supervising the foreign trade activities of their enterprises. They will participate in the enterprises' export earnings to ensure that their decisions will be based on economic criteria.

In addition, the regional administrations have been granted greater influence over the foreign trade activities of enterprises in their regions. Just as reform of public finance is giving regional administrations a direct share in the region's revenue, they are also to receive a clearly defined share of foreign currency receipts.

Finally, enterprises and enterprise associations have been given some influence over foreign trade decisions. They can take part in contract negotiations with foreign counterparts and possibly conclude agreements themselves; in certain cases they too may retain part of their foreign exchange earnings, along with the industry ministries and regional administrations.

A   Central foreign trade bodies

172. Let us first examine the foreign trade bodies at central level and the institutional changes that have occurred. The most important bodies of this kind are the newly-formed Ministry of Foreign Economic Relations and Trade (which sprang from the Ministry of Foreign Trade), its subordinate foreign trade corporations and the corresponding corporations set up by the industrial ministries. Financial and foreign exchange matters fall within the jurisdiction of the Bank of China and a number of newly-established financial institutions such as the State General Administration of Exchange Control, the China International Trust and Investment Corporation (CITIC) and the China Investment Bank. Finally, there are yet other central institutions and agencies of significance for foreign trade, such as the People's Insurance Company and the General Administration of the P.R. China for Inspection of Import and Export Commodities.

a)   The Ministry of Foreign Economic Relations and Trade

173. The main tasks of the Ministry of Foreign Economic Relations and Trade are outlined below. It co-ordinates the foreign trade plans of the industrial ministries and regional administrations and draws up the national foreign trade plan. As in the past, it has direct responsibility for imports and exports of specified goods (see below) and of plant and equipment whose value exceeds amounts laid down for each industry. The following product groups probably come under this heading (either as imports or as exports): complete factories, large items of machinery, steel products, crude oil and petroleum products, coal, tin, tungsten, antimony, cotton, fibres, rice, raw silk, pigs' bristles and

pigs intestines, feathers and vegetable oils. In the case of exports the goods are mainly those in which China has a significant position as a seller on the world market or which are particularly scarce on the domestic market.[1][2]

The Ministry must also ensure that the composition of imports by the industry ministries, regional administrations or, inasfar as this applies, enterprises themselves is consistent with the development priorities laid down by the economic policymakers. Where exports of goods not under its direct control are concerned, the Ministry gives the industry ministries, regional administrations and, where applicable, enterprises binding export quotas in keeping with export policy priorities or simply issues them with guidelines.

In addition, the Ministry is responsible for setting the prices of exported goods. It fixes the prices of goods it exports on its own account; for other products it issues price formation guidelines or in some cases sets a range within which industry ministries, regional administrations or possibly enterprises can set the most advantageous price having view to market conditions. Although over the medium term price-setting powers are also to be decentralised, at present there is still (or perhaps again) a tendency towards "uniformity" in export prices. It is feared that if this were not the case regional administrations would undercut each other in competing for customers on world markets and thus cause a deterioration in the terms of trade. The Ministry of Foreign Economic Relations and Trade has set up control offices in the main export harbours of Shanghai, Dalian, Tianjin and Guangzhou so that it can better monitor merchandise trade with the rest of the world.

The competence of the Ministry of Foreign Economic Relations and Trade also extends to the approval of equity and contractual joint ventures if their capital exceeds a certain threshold and the facilitation and intermediation of transactions.

1 Exceptions are possible, see, for example, paragraph 197.
2 Cf. WANG Shouchun, LI Kanghua: Waimao tizhi de gaige, in: HU Qiaomu (ed.): Zhongguo Baike Nianjian, loc. cit., p. 213.

174. The Ministry of Foreign Economic Relations and Trade was created in early 1982 by amalgamating the Ministry of Foreign Trade, the Import-Export Commission, the Foreign Investment Control Commission and the Ministry of Economic Relations with Foreign Countries.[1] In the course of the reforms some of the functions performed previously by these bodies were delegated to lower levels, but their other responsibilities passsed to the Ministry of Foreign Economic Relations and Trade.

As details of the new Ministry's duties have yet to be announced, a look back at the institutions it replaces can provide us with further information.

175. Until the advent of the reforms at the end of the seventies the Ministry of Foreign Trade had sole responsibility for foreign trade. It planned, co-ordinated and monitored all import and export business. Among other things, it was also responsible for the customs service and quality control for both imports and exports.[2] It conducted its business activities through special commercial bodies, the national foreign trade corporations, which were organised according to industries and had a monopoly over imports and exports of their particular categories of goods. There were eight foreign trade corporations in all; most of them probably still exist under the Ministry of Foreign Economic Relations and Trade:[3]

---

1 With regard to the reform of the foreign trade machinery see WIESE-GART, Kurt: Auch in der Außenwirtschaft soll der Wildwuchs wegge-schnitten werden, in: Handelsblatt, 13.4.1982.

2 Cf. DONNITHORNE, Audrey: China's Economic System, London 1967, pp. 321 et seqq.

3 The number of foreign trade corporations fluctuated with successive moves to restructure the economy. There were six such companies at the end of the fifties, but their number rose to thirteen in the sixties as a result of the reorganisation of responsibilities. During the seventies the number was again reduced. On this point see WEGGEL, Oskar: Das Außenhandelsrecht der VR China, Baden-Baden 1976, pp. 172 et seqq.

China National Cereals, Oils and Foodstuffs Import and Export Corporation;

China National Native Produce and Animal By-Products Imports and Export Corporation;

China National Textiles Import and Export Corporation;

China National Light Industrial Products Import and Export Corporation;

China National Chemicals Import and Export Corporation;

China National Machinery Import and Export Corporation;

China National Metals and Minerals Import and Export Corporation;

China National Technical Import Corporation.

There were also the following service companies, which were under the control of the Ministry of Foreign Trade:

China National Complete Plant Exportation Corporation;

China National Foreign Trade Packaging Corporation;

China National Foreign Trade Transportation Corporation;

China National Chartering Corporation.

Until the time of the reform the foreign trade corporations were the only official agencies entitled to negotiate and sign contracts with foreign companies. They bought up the domestic products specified in the foreign trade plan and sold them to contracting parties abroad and similarly obtained abroad the imports stated in the foreign trade plan and sold them to domestic trading companies or direct to production units. The financial side of the deals was conducted via accounts at the Bank of China, which was subordinate to the People's Bank of China and the only financial institution empowered to handle foreign business. The national foreign trade corporations had a number of regional branches. These were responsible to both the (national) foreign trade corporations and the foreign trade bureaux of the regional administrations. However, the influence that the regional administrations could bring to bear was usually very limited, as although the foreign trade bureaux were formally responsible to them, in fact they were an extension of the Ministry of Foreign Trade. (This did not prevent administrative bodies in the more highly developed regions exercising stronger influence over the foreign trade bureaux, at least during certain phases of their development.)

176. The Import-Export Commission and the Foreign Investment Control Commission, which are now part of the Ministry of Foreign Economic Relations and Trade but were independent in the days of its predecessor, were founded at the end of 1979 in connection with the authorisation of foreign direct investment. They were responsible for authorising joint ventures and other forms of foreign direct investment and were also consulted where imports of major plant were involved. [1]

Finally, the Ministry of Economic Relations with Foreign Countries had responsibility for the development aid that China grants to other countries.

177. The amalgamation of the Ministry of Foreign Trade, the two Commissions and the Ministry of Economic Relations with Foreign Countries to form the new Ministry of Foreign Economic Relations and Trade is designed to create the institutional conditions in which uniform criteria will be applied to foreign trade decisions whereas in the past the various bodies involved may have been pursuing different objective. As some of the responsibilities in this field have now been delegated to other bodies at the central and regional levels (in some instances even to enterprises), the Ministry hopes to be able to concentrate better on its remaining functions.

---

1   They were established by a decision of the State Council of 30 July
    1979. Cf. Woguo renmin daibiao dahui changwu weiyuanhui guanyu sheli
    waiguo touzi guanli weiyuanhui, jinchukou guanli weiyuanhiu he renmin
    mingdan de jueding, in: Renmin Ribao, 31.7.1979.

The new Ministry consists of eleven departments,[1] two research institutes, the China Council for the Promotion of international Trade and the General Administration of Customs. The Ministry also has direct control over fifteen foreign trade corporations.[2]

b) Industrial ministries

178. The transfer of decision making powers to industrial ministries is designed to make greater use of their knowledge of actual production conditions than in the past. Before the reforms the representatives of individual ministries were admittedly brought into negotiations between foreign trade corporations and foreign counterparts, but they were basically responsible for technical matters while the representatives of the foreign trade corporation took care of the business side. Final decisions were taken by the foreign trade corporations, which all too often disregarded the legitimate reservations and material interests of the industrial ministries.

179. At the end of the seventies selected industrial ministries were permitted to establish their own foreign trade corporations. The first corporation of this kind was the China National Machinery and Equipment Corporation, which was set up by the First Ministry of Machine-Building. Its management is composed of delegates from this ministry and from the Ministry of Foreign Trade (now the Ministry of Foreign

1 The departments are as follows: 3 regional departments (Eastern Europe; Asia and Africa; Western Europe, America and Oceania) and 8 other departments responsible for: legal affairs; the administration of foreign trade; imports and exports (co-ordination of the foreign trade corporations); development aid (Chinese development aid to other countries); economic co-operation abroad (e.g. the execution of building projects abroad, joint ventures abroad); foreign investment (all forms) of foreign capital participation, intergovernmental agreements, loans from international organisations); import and export of technology (complete technical plant); international relations (economic and technical co-operation with international organisations). Cf. TANG Ren: Zhongguo duiwai jingji maoyibu jiqi shuxia jigou, in: Jingji Daobao, 31.5.1982, pp. 16 et seqq.

2 These are primarily the corporations listed above and a number of others created when the responsibilities of the former corporations were divided up. Cf. TANG Ren, loc. cit.

Economic Relations and Trade) which sees this as a way of maintaining its influence. Soon afterwards other industrial ministries also set up foreign trade corporations, so that by the end of 1980 they already numbered seventeen.

180. The corporations can establish contact with foreign firms and negotiate about imports and exports. Presumably they are also empowered to sign contracts, provided they remain within their import and export quotas laid down in the plan.

As they receive a share of their foreign currency earnings, there is an incentive for them to export as much as possible, even if they exceed any export quotas they have been set. In that event they would earn more foreign exchange than laid down in the plan and could consequently import more than envisaged in the plan. This demonstrates that deviations from the plan are almost preprogrammed as a result of decentralisation and participation in foreign currency earnings. From the point of view of the economic policymakers, however, it is important that such deviations do not conflict with the development priorities or impair the state's "foreign trade monopoly". As a safeguard, a plethora of guidelines, regulations and codes of conduct have been issued for each of the foreign trade corporations. They are so numerous that even Chinese specialists find it difficult to gain an overall impression.

Besides commercial transactions, the foreign trade corporations of industrial ministries can usually also enter into commission processing agreements, engage in compensatory trade and become partners of foreign firms in joint ventures in China or even abroad.

181. Industry ministries are also permitted to set up service companies that operate abroad or undertake work in China for foreigners. For example, the Ministry of Communications established the China Communication Import-Export Service Corporation, which also undertakes assignments for foreigners, and the Ministry of Railways founded the China Railway Foreign Service Corporation, which offers advertising facilities fo foreign firms. (Like the foreign trade corporations, these

service companies are required to keep separate accounts and they operate on a profit basis.)

182. More recently (May 1982) an industrial ministry and its subordinate enterprises have been turned into a corporation and as such can play a part in foreign trade transactions. The ministry in question was the 6th Ministry of Machine-Building responsible for shipbuilding (paragraph 113), which now heads the China State Shipbuilding Corporation.

The China State Shipbuilding Corporation seems to have been granted wider powers to arrange its foreign trade relations than the foreign trade corporations of industrial ministries. For instance, it appears to be free to set the export prices of its ships.

183. Owing to the provisions for participation in foreign currency earnings, the foreign trade corporations of the industrial ministries (and the China State Shipbuilding Corporation, which is permitted to retain its entire foreign currency earnings, according to members of the company) have it in their power to increase their foreign currency balance at the Bank of China by expanding their export activities. However, as the central government generally does not allocate them any foreign exchange to pay for their imports and they are thus obliged to earn whatever they require, their sense of responsibility has also been increased.

Little has become known about the form that foreign currency sharing takes. As a rule, the central government's previous foreign exchange allocations to industry ministries seem to serve as a guide in determining the relative shares. However, the authorities also want to make the level depend on the export volume of the preceding year in order to create an incentive to expand exports.[1] The relevant development priorities will also be a determining factor. Hence it can be assumed that foreign trade corporations selling the products of heavy industry

1 Cf. WANG Shouchun, LI Kanghua: Waimao tizhi de gaige, loc.cit., p. 213.

will be allowed relatively low participation rates, because at present China's economic policymakers do not want large-scale imports for the development of heavy industry.

c) Central financial institutions

184. Changes have been made in the central financial institutions in order to cope with the additional financing tasks connected with the increased use of foreign capital and the diversification of capital flows. The Bank of China, which had hitherto performed mainly administrative functions, has been given some latitude for commercial activities and has become more flexible as a result. At the same time the Bank surrendered one important administrative task, namely exchange control, to the newly established State General Administration of Exchange Control. The government has also established the China International Trust and Investment Corporation (CITIC) primarily as a contact point for potential foreign investors and the China Investment Bank for matters relating to lending by international organisations.

Bank of China

185. The Bank of China is the most important financial institution for all of China's import and export trade. Until the beginning of 1979 it was subordinate to the People's Bank of China. When the growing volume of external trade led to an expansion in its duties, it was placed under the direct control of the State Council, which amounts to an enhancement of its position within the administrative machine.[1]

186. Without exception, all economic entities and government agencies that maintain business relations with parties abroad must hold accounts at the Bank of China.[2] All foreign currency transactions are effected via these accounts.

1 Cf. Beijing Rundschau, No. 29, 1981.
2 Cf. Ta Kung Pao, 7.1.1982.

The Bank of China acts as an agency of the state administration in that it allocates the foreign exchange needed for specific import schemes to central and regional authorities, corporations and enterprises as directed by the planning and economic bodies. It is also responsible for supervision in an area considered to be very "sensitive": it ensures that public authorities, corporations and enterprises use "their" foreign currency earned from exports only for projects that are consistent with the country's development priorities. Too strict a control over the use of foreign exchange combined with protracted approval procedures can easily cause these bodies to lose interest in earning foreign exchange. However, for various reasons which include the "artificiality" of price relations, the government believes that the profitability considerations of individual enterprises alone do not necessarily lead to optimum results for the economy as a whole and therefore wishes to monitor the use of scarce foreign exchange.

Like the People's Bank, the Bank of China has been performing some of the functions of a commercial bank since the end of the seventies in that it grants loans, including loans in foreign currencies such as US dollars, Hong Kong dollars, Japanese yen, pounds sterling and Deutsche Mark.[1] The borrower's ability to repay the loan is an important criterion, but the Bank also has to ensure that the projects to be financed by its loans are consistent with the overall economic priorities. Since mid 1982 the Bank of China has also undertaken export credit financing.[2] Finally, it can take up loans abroad in foreign currency and raise foreign equity capital.

The decentralisation measures will also entail the delegation of powers within the Bank of China; subject to certain limitations, regional branches will be able to undertake financial transactions without refer-

1 Cf. China Daily, 6.3.1982.

2 The fact that exports could not be financed on an interim basis by means of bank loans was long an obstacle to the direct acceptance of large export contracts by Chinese enterprises themselves. The first substantial export credit financed by the Bank of China concerned a US-$ 30 million contract for the supply of four freighters. Cf. The Wall Street Journal, 13.5.1982.

ence to head office. The extent of their powers of decision on the degree of autonomy enjoyed by the region in matters of external trade and hence on the amount of foreign currency it administers. For example, the Bank's branch in Shanghai has greater independence than those in other regions that are less important from the point of view of foreign trade.

State General Administration of Exchange Control

187. The State General Administration of Exchange Control, which was split off from the Bank of China at the end of the seventies, is a purely administrative body under the direct control of the State Council. It is responsible for setting exchange rates, drafting exchange control regulations and taking other foreign exchange measures.[1] It also co-operates with other government agencies (the Planning Commission, the Economic Commission and the Ministry of Finance) and the Bank of China in drafting the short and long-term foreign exchange receipts and expenditure plans.

China International Trust and Investment Corporation (CITIC)

188. The main responsibility of the CITIC, which was established at the end of 1979 and is under the direct control of the State Council, is the importation of foreign capital and foreign technology. It is an important point of initial contact for foreign investors. It therefore plays a central role in the establishment of equity joint ventures; foreign companies can approach it for information on potential Chinese partners and agreements negotiated between foreign and Chinese parties must be vetted by the CITIC on behalf of the State Council - in this respect it performs a sovereign function. The CITIC can also participate in joint ventures itself. For example, it is a partner in a leasing company established jointly with the Beijing Machinery and Equipment Corporation and a

1   Cf. Renmin Ribao, 4.12.1981.

Japanese company. It is also empowered to raise loans abroad[1] and issue bonds. At the beginning of 1982 it issued bonds to the value of 10 billion yen in the Tokyo capital market.[2]

The importance of the CITIC will doubtless continue to grow as may be seen from the intended increase in its capital base from 200 to 600 million Yuan.[3]

China Investment Bank

189. The China Investment Bank was founded at the end of 1981. It has a capital base of 4 billion Yuan, which is extremely large in comparison with that of the Bank of China (1 billion Yuan).[4]

According to the information available, it is under the control of the Ministry of Finance. Its main functions seem to be to administer loans granted by international organisations and, related to this, to award loans for domestic investment projects. According to the sources available, the loans it grants are primarily for schemes with a maximum value of US-$ 5 million.[5] The Bank is required to base its assessment of investment projects on the investment criteria worked out by the World Bank. In the past China took most of her investment decisions in the light of general development considerations; precise criteria of viability were not applied. In the course of the present change-over from the previous system of grants to a credit financing basis the authorities are seeking suitable lending criteria. The decision that the newly-formed Investment Bank shall take the investment criteria of the World Bank as a standard is doubtless an interesting development.

1 The CITIC uses the funds raised abroad to grant loans to domestic enterprises. According to information from Hong Kong, the CITIC lent Chinese enterprises a total of 500 million Yuan at short and medium term in 1981. Cf. Far Eastern Economic Review, 28.5.1982.

2 Cf. China Daily, 10.12.1982.

3 Cf. Internationale Wirtschaft, 18.3.1982.

4 Cf. The China Business Review, January-February 1982, p. 5.

5 Cf. Quoted from the China Business Review, loc. cit.

Other important bodies in the foreign trade field

190. The state insurance company (the People's Insurance Company of China)[1] recently broadened the scope of its activities and therefore assumed greater importance for foreign businessmen. Hitherto it had insured only risks for imports and exports in transit and activities at trade fairs. It has now begun to cover the risks of foreign capital involved in joint ventures (a policy issued by the People's Insurance Company of China is obligatory under the Law on Joint Ventures), compensation trade and the exploration work of foreign oil companies. The company even insures against loss or damage caused by strikes, riots or expropriation.[2] In order to increase potential customer's confidence in the Company, it has concluded numerous re-insurance contracts with insurance companies of other countries and signed agreements with foreign governments on the assumption of investments risks (USA and Sweden and so far; negotiations with other countries are proceeding).[3] Furthermore, at the end of 1980 the People's Insurance Company set up a joint venture with an American insurance company, the first of its kind.

One of the possible attractions of the Company for foreign partners lies in the fact that where losses have occurred in, say, the production sphere it ensures that production is restarted as quickly as possible by arranging itself for the replacement of damaged machinery. In this way the lost production and hence the Company's own liability are kept to a minimum and the foreign partner is spared the protracted bureaucratic procedures involved in acquiring replacement plant.

---

1   The People's Insurance Company has two subsidiaries, the China Insurance Company Limited and the Taiping Insurance Company Limited. Hitherto the subsidiary companies operated outside the People's Republic of China, mainly in Hong Kong, Macao und Singapore. Cf. WANG Yung-Ming: China's Insurance and her Foreign Trade, in: China's Foreign Trade and its Management, Hong Kong 1978, pp. 106 et seqq.

2   Cf. Renmin Ribao, 11.1.1981.

3   Cf. Blick durch die Wirtschaft, 16.4.1982.

191. The China National Import and Export Commodities Inspection Corporation checks the quality of imported and exported goods. It is responsible to the General Administration of the P.R. China for Inspection of Import and Export Commodities, which was set up in 1980 to establish suitable methods and criteria of inspection and to draft appropriate legislation. (Before 1980 the inspection of goods fell within the ambit of the Ministry of Foreign Trade.)

192. The Foreign Economic and Trade Arbitration Commission was also established in 1980; this body is under the direct control of the State Council and replaces the former arbitration commission belonging to the China Council for the Promotion of International Trade (CCPIT, see below). It has jurisdiction over disputes in connection with loans, joint ventures, compensatory trade, commission processing deals and patents.[1]

In matters concerning the place of arbitration, the law to be applied in arbitration proceedings or the official language to be used the Chinese are now more prepared to follow international practice.[2] There is an increasing readiness to sanction a jurisdiction outside China, an apparent inclination to use the United Nations' arbitration rules as a basis for proceedings and a move away from the previous insistence on Chinese as the only permissible language.[3]

193. The China Council for the Promotion of International Trade (CCPIT), which was mentioned above in connection with the Arbitration Commission, played an important role in the history of the People's Republic of China so long as she maintained diplomatic relations with only a handful of countries. At htat time the CCPIT had the task of

---

1 Cf. XNA, 17.7.1980.

2 The legal issues arising from conflicts between the interests of foreign investors and those of the host country are by no means confined to China. See KEBSCHULL, Dietrich, NAINI, Ahmad, STEGGER, Manfred, inter alia: Industrialisierung im Nord-Süd-Dialog - Vorschläge zur 3. Generalkonferenz von UNIDO und Bewertung des Verlaufs, Munich 1980, pp. 88 et seqq.

3 In this regard see REN Jianxin: China's Economic and Trade Arbitration, in: China's Foreign Trade, No. 2, 1981, pp. 4 et seqq.

establishing trade links with countries with which China did not have diplomatic relations. By the mid seventies China had won diplomatic recognition from practically all her trading partners, so that the CCPIT turned its attention mainly to fostering contacts with overseas committees, chambers of commerce and similar official institutions in foreign countries; it organised trade fairs and exhibitions (such as the Canton trade fair) and operated mainly in the field of trade promotion. Nothing is yet known about the present functions of the CCPIT or its institutional status since the reforms.

B   Regional foreign trade bodies

194. At the regional administrative level the provinces (including the centrally-administered municipalities) and a very few cities and districts have been granted wider powers with regard to the export (and import) of goods, services and capital.

The widest powers have been granted to the coastal regions,[1] among which the cities of Beijing, Shanghai and Tianjin and above all the provinces of Guangdong and Fujian occupy a leading position. The regions have been permitted to set up their own foreign trade bodies so that they can fulfil their growing responsibilities. The central authorities did not lay down any binding organisational structure - none exists so far either for foreign trade or for the domestic economy, as stated above. As a result, extremely diverse solutions have evolved so that it is very difficult to categorise the different administrative ar-

1 The coastal regions are more highly developed than the inland regions, a fact that is to be exploited in extending China's foreign trade relations. About 45 per cent of all industrial plant in the country are concentrated in the three cities mentioned above and in the provinces Liaoning, Hebei, Shandong, Jiangsu, Zhejiang, Fujian, Guangdong and Guangxi. In 1980 these regions generated 57 per cent of the country's gross agricultural output and 62 per cent of her industrial production and produced about 75 per cent of all export goods. Cf. Fahui yanhai diqu youshi - jiaqiang duiwai jingji maoyi, in: Renmin Ribao, 17.1.1982. With regard to the future role of the coastal regions see ZHANG Peiji: Stick to open Policy and expand Foreign Trade, in: Economic Reporter, No. 5, 1982, pp. 2 et seqq.

rangements in the various regions. Nevertheless, some general conclusions can be drawn about the relationships between the various bodies and corporations themselves and about their fields of competence. (For particulars on the special economic zones, see paragraph 204).

195. Under the reforms an initially small number of provinces established a so-called Import-Export Commission to represent regional interests as a parallel to the Foreign Trade Bureau, which had previously enjoyed sole responsibility for the province's foreign trade affairs and was generally subordinate to the Ministry of Foreign Trade (paragraph 175). Other titles also occur; in Fujian for example, it is called the Import-Export Bureau. In some provinces the Foreign Trade Bureau was subsequently abolished, so that the regional Import-Export Commission not only had to represent regional interests but also implement directives from the Ministry of Foreign Trade concerning their region, such as import and export quotas of important goods. In regions where the bureau and the commission continue to exist by side, the former is generally responsible for the implementation of central government requirements while the latter looks after regional interests in the foreign trade field.

In their capacity as representatives of the interests of their region, the regional import-export commissions have established corporations specialising in certain tasks to carry out foreign trade transactions. These include foreign trade corporations and service companies that also undertake overseas business and investment companies. (In some instances "co-ordination corporations" have also been set up to orchestrate the different operations of these corporations.) These corporations owned solely by the regions generally exist side by side with the regional branches of national corporations (foreign trade corporations and service companies of the Ministry of Foreign Economic Relations and Trade and the industrial ministries; the CITIC). There are also cases in which the branches have been "uncoupled" from the national corporations and placed under the control of the regional import-export commissions or in which powers over individual goods of importance for the region has been transferred from the branches to the newly-formed regional corporations. (For example, in Jiangsu - one of the leading provinces for silk production - the national foreign trade corporation's branch responsible for textiles ceded its powers over the export of silk to the Jiangsu Silk Branch.)

196. Regional government bodies and their corporations are granted a share in their export earnings as an incentive to intensify their foreign trade. In most cases they receive a predetermined percentage, which differs from region to region. Special arrangements appear to have been made for the provinces of Guangdong and Fujian, as they were too in the domestic sphere (paragraph 94); they are required to transfer a fixed amount of foreign exchange to the central authorities each year and can retain any excess.[1]

The regional foreign exchange quotas are generally related to the foreign exchange allocations the regions received for imports before the reforms, usually in a particular "base year". (Obviously this is not possible in the case of the newly-established regional corporations.) Consequently, those regions that previously received relatively high foreign exchange allocations will be in a better position to increase their foreign currency earnings. The regions "favoured" in this way are mainly the provinces on the east coast, which exported considerable quantities in the past and were allocated comparatively large amounts of foreign currency to develop their export capacity. They thus have the opportunity to modernise and expand their production facilities more quickly than inland regions by using foreign capital. The Chinese leadership accepts the at least temporary widening of regional disparities that this will bring (paragraph 96), because they hope that the concentration of foreign capital goods and technology in a small number of regions will produce greater overall growth in the medium term; it is expected that growth stimuli will spread very quickly from the more

---

1   The authorities are contemplating allowing the two provinces to retain all their foreign currency receipts for a limited period; sources: notes by WIESEGART, Kurt on his conversations with members of the Ministry of Foreign Economic Relations and Trade.

highly developed regions to the other areas of the country. Examples of how this might occur are already available; purely Chinese joint ventures have been established between regions that have capital but abundant natural resources.[1]

197. The jurisdiction of the various national and regional foreign trade corporations to be found in a region are generally segregated by regulation. There is occasionally some overlap due more to the lack of clear concepts and to difficulties in defining business activities for administrative purposes than to the intention to permit competition between the corporations. (Different regions' corporations in the same field may, however, compete against one another.)

In principle, the branches of the foreign trade corporations of the Ministry of Foreign Economic Relations and Trade are responsible for the export of commodities such as petroleum, coal, antimony, rice etc. (paragraph 173), produced in the region, but exceptions are possible. For example, the coal-rich province of Shanxi has set up its own foreign trade corporation which buys up the output of the "provincially owned" coal mines in excess of the plan target.[2] Foreign trade corporations of the industrial ministries generally export goods produced in the region's plant that are under the control of the relevant ministry. Goods and industrial products that do not fall within the competence of the Ministry for Foreign Economic Relations and Trade or the industrial ministries may be purchased and exported by the regional foreign trade corporations.

---

1 For example, some of the regions that are poor in energy are participating in the development of coal deposits in the coal-rich province of Shanxi; cf. XNA, 4.8.1982. Shanghai, Tianjin and Jiangsu province are helping finance certain industrial projects in the inland regions of Guanxi and Yunnan; cf. XNA, 6.8.1982. With regard to possible forms of interregional co-operation, see WANG Yihe, loc. cit., pp. 92 et seqq.

2 The Shanxi Coal Export Corporation was established at the end of 1980. It is responsible not only for the export of coal but also for the involvement of foreign capital in the development of the local coal sector; cf. XNA, 23.12.1980.

198. The scope for central and regional bodies to earn their "own" foreign exchange is greatly affected by the products the various corporations are allowed to handle and by the administrative level to which plant are attached. The corporations are therefore constantly attempting to gain control over products that yield large quantities of foreign exchange. (The clash of interests is particularly marked in the case of petroleum. The development of the offshore reserves with the aid of foreign capital has been entrusted to the (central) China National Offshore Oil Corporation, but the regions with oil reserves of their own have announced their interest in sharing in the expected foreign currency earnings.)

199. Regional administrations have been given considerable powers of decision over goods (quantities, qualities, etc.) for which they have export responsibilities. This does not prevent the Ministry of Foreign Economic Relations and Trade from laying down guidelines for the overall volume of their exports and for exports of particular goods or even from setting quotas. In addition, customs measures are used to steer exports in the desired direction.

200. They usually have independent powers of decision with regard to imports, for which they have to pay with their "own" foreign exchange (this generally applies to plant under their control; imports for enterprises governed by the industrial ministries must be carried out by the corporations of the ministries involved). Nevertheless, they must adhere to the national development priorities, which are enforced partly by customs measures; imports of major plant must be cleared with the higher authorities.

201. There are fewer problems in dividing the overseas trade responsibilities of service companies at different administrative levels because the range of exportable services is still very narrow and can easily be classified. For example, Shanghai offers foreign businessmen consultancy services through the Jinjiang Service Center for Overseas Business

People[1] and the Guangdong Manpower Corporation offers to find labour for construction projects abroad.[2]

202. Capital exports by regional administrations - for example, in connection with joint ventures between regional corporations and foreign enterprises abroad or for the establishment of sales offices abroad to open up overseas markets for the products of the region - are possible in principle, but in practice very few cases have occured. Regional bodies and corporations must seek authorisation from the central agencies.

203. By contrast, capital imports by regional administrations have already reached significant proportions. The regional investment corpo-rations set up so far in the regions (and centrally administered munici-palities) are responsible for raising foreign loans and risk capital for joint ventures and for setting up compensatory trade and commission processing deals. Contracts are approved by the region's import-export commission or, if they exceed certain upper limits, by the central authorities (in the case of equity joint ventures it is still the central authorities that are responsible). The upper limits differ from one region to another; some provinces may decide on contractual joint ventures, compensatory trade and commission processing deals with a value of up to 1 million Yuan, but for the cities of Shanghai, Beijing and Tianjin the ceilings are 3 million Yuan and for the provinces of Guangdong and Fujian 5 million Yuan.[3]

---

1 Cf.   Internationale Wirtschaft, 21.8.1981.

2 Cf.   The China Business Review, March-April 1980, pp. 36 et seqq.

3 In addition, the regions are empowered to sign contracts relating to projects that have been agreed with the central authorities. This was the case with the 130 participation projects put out to tender at the conference for the promotion of foreign capital investment held in Canton in June 1982 (paragraph 130). In the case of these projects the ceiling has been set at US-$ 5 million for the three above-named cities and Liaoning province, and at US-$ 3 million for other cities and provinces. No upper limit at all has been imposed on the prov-inces of Guangdong and Fujian provided the projects can be integrated into the local economy. Cf. China's New Major Drive to Seek Foreign Investment, in: Economic Reporter, April 1982, p. 10.

Individual investment corporations have been empowered by the State Council to sell the province's bonds on foreign capital markets. Fujian already intends to issue bonds worth US-$ 60 million in the capital markets of Hong Kong of Japan.[1] (In the late fifties the province of Fujian and Guangdong had already sold bonds to Chinese resident abroad.)

The capital imports contractually agreed or realised in recent years by some regions under joint venture agreements, compensatory trade transactions and commission processing deals have reached substantial proportions. At the end of 1981 the value of contracts for the importation of plant and equipment in Guangdong province came to more than US-$ 2 billion,[2] the bulk of this relating to the Shenzhen special economic zone. By the same date Shanghai had received foreign capital worth some US-$ 220 million[3] and Zhejiang province a total of about US-$ 31 million.[4]

204. Special administrative organs and corporations have been set up to provide an institutional check on the greater independence that special economic zones enjoy with regard to the import or export of goods, services and capital (paragraph 164). Guangdong and Fujian provinces (in which the special economic zones established so far situated) each have an Administration for Special Economic Zones, which is theoretically under the control of the provincial region but has relatively broad powers in relation to the development of the zone with the help of foreign capital. They control co-ordination corporations for the trade, service and capital transactions of the respective zones. In Shenzhen the Guangdong Provincial Special Economic Zone Development Corporation is responsible for co-ordination while in Xiamen this role is fulfilled by the Xiamen Construction and Development Corporation. They are also contact organisations for interested foreign businessmen and establish

1   Cf.   The Journal of Commerce, 2.4.1982.
2   Cf.   The Wall Street Journal, 2.7.1982.
3   Cf.   XNA,   14.7.1982.
4   Cf.   XNA,   9.7.1982.

overseas contacts for Chinese enterprises. Below the co-ordination corporations come corporations specialising in certain types of business; thus in Shenzhen there are firms responsible for finding premises and personnel.

205. The delegation of powers of decision to regional bodies and their participation in profits and foreign exchange earnings have helped break down rigid bureaucratic structures and spur local initiative. The conscious exploitation of local interest in profit has stimulated activity, but in some cases this has had less desirable effects on the economy as a whole. The Chinese leadership has taken various steps to prevent adverse developments in future and to achieve better overall results. Direct central control over some important areas such as exports of important products (quantities and prices) and imports of large plant has been strengthened; the Ministry of Foreign Economic Relations and Trade has set up "representative offices" in the various provinces so that it can better perform its supervisory functions. (In Guangdong this representative office is also responsible for supervising the province's special economic zones.) Instruments for manipulating flows of goods indirectly (such as customs measures) are being developed so that centrally determined priorities can also be enforced in a decentralised economy.

China is also attempting to reduce the now apparent barriers and the inefficiency of administrative control and to clarify the jurisdiction of the various levels and corporations. The ultimate determining factor will be the organisational reforms adopted in the domestic economy. Nonetheless, complicated administrative arrangements will be unavoidable for many years to come. All the authorities are seeking to do at present is to apportion responsibilities in a comprehensible and economically sound manner.

Finally, steps have been taken to overcome the limits on the powers of regional bodies by establishing economic co-operation among different regions. An example in this field is the establishment of the China South West Energy Development Corporation by the three ministries responsible for coal, the railways and transport, the governments of the provinces of Guizhou, Yunnan, Guangdong and Guangxi and the Bank of China to exploit the coal deposits in Guizhou province (in the Liupanshui coalfield). The ministries, the regions and the Bank want to co-operate in order to share the tasks that arise from exploitation of the coalfield, including the development of an infrastructure. The new energy corporation is negotiating with firms from the United States and elsewhere that wish to participate in the project.[1]

C   Enterprises and mergers

206. In the external sector the emphasis of decentralisation lies on the delegation of powers not to enterprises as in the domestic economy but to regional administration, at least initially. Nonetheless, selected enterprises have already been given the opportunity to represent their own interests in the importation and exportation of goods and capital.

207. A small number of enterprises have been permitted to conclude export contracts on their own authority. These include 25 engineering factories. Some large enterprises such as the steel mill in Wuhan may even establish their own foreign trade corporations. (In the first six months of its existence the Wuhan Metallurgical Import Export Corporation had already signed export contracts worth US-$ 100 million.[2] Certain enterprise associations are also allowed to sell their products abroad independently. These enterprises and enterprise associations are not generally from traditional Chinese exporting industries; they are mainly enterprises from sectors with overcapacity (heavy industry) or in which a rapid expansion of exports is regarded as particularly desirable (such as high-value products).

---

1 Cf. China Trade Report, No. 4 and 5, 1982; The China Business Review, March-April 1982, p. 33.
2 Cf. Wuhan zhijie jingjying chukou maoyi, in: Renmin Ribao, 5.9.1981.

Enterprises' ties with foreign markets have also been strengthened by encouraging them to provide staff and capital to foreign trade corporations. Finally, a few plant may take part in export negotiations between foreign trade corporations and foreign buyers and represent their own interests. Moreover, the foreign trade corporations want to stop laying down supply quotas for enterprises or enterprise associations. Administrative directives are to be replaced by contracts negotiated with the enterprises involved.[1]

Enterprises in the special economic zones and joint ventures set up outside the zones occupy a special position as far as the export of their products is concerned. In these enterprises the foreign partner is usually obliged to assume full responsibility for marketing the output.

208. Those enterprises and enterprise associations that are allowed to sign export contracts with foreign buyers in their own right generally receive a share of the foreign exchange earned. The amount of foreign exchange retained by enterprises in this way is negligible in comparison with the sum earned from total exports as the number of enterprises exporting independently is still very small.

The remaining enterprises and enterprise associations that produce goods for export receive a share of their profits in domestic currency. The de facto devaluation of the Yuan resulting from the introduction of a special settlement rate (paragraph 137) has led to a trend rise in export earnings expressed in Yuan. Amongst other things, this takes into account the fact that the prime costs of enterprises producing goods for export are higher than those of firms manufacturing comparable products for the domestic market because of the more stringent quality requirements.

---

1 Cf. PAN Enqi: Ban hao chukou zhuanchang geng hao de wei jingji tiao-zheng fuwu, in: Caimao Jingji, No. 3, 1981, pp. 26-27, reprinted in Waimao Jingji, No. 9, 1981, pp. 82 et seqq.

209. The number of enterprises that are free to conclude export contracts is small, but even fewer can negotiate independently for imports. Until now only a very few firms in the electronics industry and the textile sector in Guangdong province have been given the opportunity to purchase inputs, plant and equipment independently on the world market, and then subject to a time limit.[1] The foreign currency they need for this purpose must be earned by exporting. Apart from these, the vast majority of enterprises that are paid a share of their foreign exchange earnings are not empowered to import goods without consulting higher authority and the Bank of China. The economic policymakers still hold the view that scarce foreign currency can be used more economically and sensibly from the development point of view if it is managed by administrative bodies working in collaboration with the Bank of China.

Enterprises in the special economic zones and joint ventures again constitute an exception; if the contracts by which they were established provide for imports of inputs, machinery or plant, the enterprises may make the necessary imports although they must themselves generate the foreign currency required.

210. In the last few years the introduction of import and export duties (paragraphs 133 and 138) has created important safeguards to ensure that export and import transactions by individual enterprises do not conflict with national economic policy. It may be assumed that the leadership is contemplating cautious reforms and considering allowing a slightly larger circle of enterprises direct contacts with suppliers and purchasers on the world market.

211. In principle enterprises and enterprise associations are permitted to export capital if, for example, they wish to found joint ventures abroad with foreign partners or set up marketing organisations overseas. The authorisation procedures are laborious, however. Very few enterprises have availed themselves of this possibility so far.

1 Cf. Finanz- und Wirtschaftsspiegel, Internationale Wirtschaft, No. 96, 21.5.1982.

212. Nonetheless, there are some firms that have raised capital abroad by taking up loans, albeit not without state approval. For example, the Yanshan Petrochemical General Corporation of the Peking oil refinery obtained a foreign loan of about US-$ 50 million to finance the importation of plant; the loan was guaranteed by the Beijing Investment Corporation.[1] At present this is till the exception, however; enterprises normally submit their import applications to the Bank of China, Which provides the necessary foreign exchange after examining and approving the proposals. Once again, joint ventures occupy a special position. With the approval of the Bank of China they may open accounts with foreign banks and obtain finance independently, subject to the prevailing exchange control regulations.

Enterprises can also obtain foreign capital by concluding compensatory trade or commission processing deals with foreign partners or give the latter a direct capital interest by founding a joint venture. However, all these possibilities require consultation with the competent bodies and approval by higher authorities - in the case of equity joint ventures this means the Ministry of Foreign Economic Relations and Trade itself. China's policymakers wish to be certain that the interests of the Chinese partner are safeguarded.

1 Cf. Vereinigte Wirtschaftsdienste, 8.7.1981.

SUMMARY

This study has examined the changes in China's development strategy and the new foreign economic policy she has pursued since the end of the seventies. The first chapter began with an exposition of the salient features of the previous development policy, the reasons for the change of direction and the new elements in the policy pursued since the change occurred. There then followed an examination of the most impor~ tant measures taken. These include the reduction of the investment ratio, comprehensive sectoral restructuring, the extension of foreign trade relations, increases in incomes and organisational reforms aimed at giving wider powers of decision to regional administrations and enter- prises.

In essence, the examination shows that the restructuring and adjust- ments associated with the change in development priorities and with the organisational reforms have not proceeded intirely smoothly so far. Many individual measures, most of them in the organisation field still need to be better co-ordinated. It also emerged that China can come to grips better with certain problems of sectoral restructuring and realise her development programme more quickly if she employs certain foreign inputs, be they capital goods, consumer goods or consultancy.

The analysis of China's new foreign trade policy in the second chapter demonstrates that in certain areas China has already been able to adjust the volume and composition of her imports to suit the new development priorities. In this field China has also made use of foreign capital in a variety of forms; she has taken up loans (at the end of 1981 her debt amounted to just under US-$ 5 billion) and obtained capital worth a further US-$--2-3 billion through joint ventures, compensatory trade and the like.

The institutional changes in the foreign trade field have been described in fairly great detail. The reform of the foreign trade apparatus is designed primarily to ensure that end users play a substantial part in decisions to import goods and capital and that export decisions are partly borne by those engaged in producing the goods in question. In this way the effectiveness of imports and exports should be enhanced at the level of the enterprise and that of the economy as a whole.

Whereas the reforms in the domestic economy have brought a large number of enterprises a fair degree of freedom to decide matters such as procurement, production and sales, in the foreign trade field only a very small number of enterprises so far have been allowed to take their own decisions regarding imports and exports. At the present stage of the reform it is still a question of giving ministries concerned with production and regional bureaux or commissions a greater say in foreign trade matters.

The delegation of foreign trade powers to industrial ministries and regional administrations - which have been permitted to establish specialised corporations to conduct foreign trade activities - and the establishment of various new institutions have created a very complex foreign trade structure with jurisdiction differing from one region to another. A highly simplified outline of the new foreign trade organisation and its functions has been drawn in order to indicate its post-reform structure.

It is conceivable that enterprises (or enterprise associations) will be given a greater say than hitherto in foreign trade matters as well, for two reasons; first, the distribution of powers of decision over foreign trade among a multitude of central and regional bodies (each receiving different shares of their profits and/or foreign currency earnings) quickly reaches the limits of economic practicality and secondly the development of a range of tariff instruments has already created some of the prerequisites for pursuading individual enterprises to reach export and import decisions that are consistent with macroeconomic priorities. However, central authorities will in any case continue to exercise direct control over important exports and imports and over capital flows and to exert indirect influence over the transfer of other goods. In reforming the system and redistributing powers accordingly, the authorities cannot be guided solely by "optimum economic conditions" (closeness to the production process, market transparency, responsibility). They will also have to take the structure of society and the behaviour of the bureaucracy into account. A reform programme that was too radical could suffer a lasting reversal if it threatened the interests of key groups.

BIBLIOGRAPHY

BOOKS AND ARTICLES

An Zuoxiang
    Guanyu woguo shiyou ziyuan de jige wenti,   in: Nengyuan, No. 2
    1982

Bolz, Klaus;   Plötz, Peter
    Erfahrungen aus der Ost-West-Kooperation, Hamburg 1974

Cao Xia
    Guding   zichan zhejiu de jige wenti, in: Caizheng Yanjiu, No. 2,
    1981

Chen Huiqin
    Jishu yinjin de fangxiang bixu zhuanbian, in: Jingji Guanli, No. 4
    1981

Chen Zhibao
    Guomin shouru fanwei de chongxin kaocha,   in: Jingji Yanjiu, No.
    4, 1981

Dong Furen;   Wang Xiangming
    Shehuizhui jingji fazhan de gao sudu wenti,   in: Jingji Yanjiu, No.
    4, 1981

Donnithorne, Audrey
    China's Economic System, London 1967

Dong Qing
    Feilüpin de chukou jiagong qu, in: Gonggye Jingji Guanli Congkan,
    No. 4, 1981,   reprinted in: Zhongguo Renmin Daxue Shubao Ziliao
    She (ed.):   Gongye Jingji, Peking, F 3, No. 12, 1981

Fang Yuan
    Woguo   nongye   xiandaihua   de   jiben   renwu   yingshi tigao danwei
    mianji chanliang,   in: Jingji Yanjiu, No. 3, 1980

Fang Zhuofen
    Lun jingji tequ de xingzhi,   in: Jingji Yanjiu, No. 6, 1981

Guo Hanbin
    Woguo   zai   guowai   kaiban   hezi   jingying qiye de jige wenti,   in:
    Jingji Cankao, No. 4, 15.2.1982, reprinted in: Zhongguo Renmin
    Daxue Shubao Ziliao She (ed.):   Maoyi Jingji, Peking, F 5,   No. 3
    1982

Gui Shiyong;   Zhou Shulian
    Lun jingji tiaozheng de mubiao, jieduan he cuoshi, in: Jingji Yanjiu,
    No. 6, 1981

Hishida, Masaharu
State Finance and Financial Reform, in: JETRO China Newsletter, October 1980

Huang Zhenqi
Dui guoying qiye kuoda jingying guanli zizhuquan jige wenti de taolun, in: Jingji Yanjiu, No. 3, 1982

Ishikawa, Shigeru
National Income and Capital Formation in Mainland China - An Examination of Official Statistics, Tokyo 1965

Ji Chongwei
Chinas Kapazität zur Aufnahme ausländischer Investitionen, in: Beijing Rundschau, No. 17, 27.4.1982

Yingyong bijiao chengbenlun zhidao woguo duiwai maoyi, zai guoji maoyizhong qude jiao hao de jingji xiaoguo, in: Waimao Jingji yu Yanjiu, Peking, No. 3, 1981, reprinted in: Zhongguo Renmin Daxue Shubao Ziliao She (ed.): Waimao Jingji, Peking, F 5, No. 3, 1982

Jiang Junchen; Zhou Chaoyang; Shen Jun
Lun shengchan he shenghuo de guanxi wenti, in: Jingji Yanjiu, No. 9, 1980

Kebschull, Dietrich; Naini, Ahmad; Stegger, Manfred u.a.
Industrialisierung im Nord-Süd-Dialog - Vorschläge zur 3. Generalkonferenz von UNIDO und Bewertung des Verlaufs, München 1980

Klenner, Wolfgang
Ordnungsprinzipien im Industrialisierungsprozeß der VR China, Hamburg 1979

Wirtschaftliche Entwicklung und strukturelle Ungleichgewichte in der Volksrepublik China, in: Osteuropa-Wirtschaft, No. 4, December 1980

Der Wandel in der Entwicklungsstrategie der VR China. Umstrukturierung und Reform der chinesischen Wirtschaft seit 1978, Hamburg 1981

Kapitalbildung und wirtschaftliche Entwicklung in der Volksrepublik China, in: Yu Cheung-Lieh (ed.): Chinas neue Wirtschaftspolitik, Frankfurt, New York 1980

Market-Economic Experiments in China's Planned Economy, in: Intereconomics, January-February 1981

Klenner, Wolfgang; Wiesegart, Kurt
Joint Ventures in the PR China, in: Intereconomics, March-April 1980

Li Chengrui
      Caizheng, xindai pingheng yu guomin jingji de zonghe pingheng, in: Jingji Yanjiu, No. 3, 1981

Li Kaixin
      An shangpin yuanze zuzhi shengchan ziliao de liutong, in: Wuzi Guanli, No. 1, 1980

Li Long
      Guanche tiaozheng da li fazhan xiaofeipin shengchan, in: Jingji Yanjiu, No. 5, 1981

Li Long; Lu Nan
      Tantan gongnongye pin jiage de jiandaocha, in: Hongqi, No. 6, 1980

Lin Zili
      Kuoda zaishengchan de jige wenti, in: Hongqi, No. 9, 1981

Ling Chen
      Shilun caitizhi gaige de zuoyong jiqi wanshan de tujing, in: Caizheng Yanjiu, No. 4, 1982

Liu Lixin; Tian Chungsheng
      Zenyang renshi yasuo jiben jianshe guimo, in: Hongqi, No. 8, 1981

Loong, P.
      Special Zones, Special Rules, in: Far Eastern Economic Review, No. 38, 12.9.1980

Lü Lüping
      Guanyu jiasu fazhan qinggongye de jige wenti, in: Jingji Yanjiu, No. 2, 1980

Pan Enqi
      Ban hao chukou zhuanchang genghao de wei jingji tiaozheng fuwu, in: Caimao Jingji, No. 3, 1981, reprinted in: Zhongguo Renmin Daxue Shubao Ziliao She (ed.): Waimao Jingji, Peking F 5, No. 9 1981

Peng Rongquan
      Di wu jiang: Jiben jianshe jihua biaoge, in: Jihua Jingji, No. 5, 1957

Ren Jianxin
      China's Foreign Economic and Trade Arbitration, in: China's Foreign Trade, No. 2, 1981

Ren Tao
      Sichuan bai ge shidian qiye su jian chengxiao de yuanyin he zai? in: Jingji Guanli, No. 12, 1979

Sai Feng
      Woguo shiyou ziyuan de qianjing yu pucha kantan renwu, in: Renmin Ribao, 16.4.1982

Shao Ying
    An shehuizhuyi jiben jingji guilü ban shi, in: Hongqi, No. 5, 1980

Smil, Vaclav
    China's Energetics: A System Analysis, in: Chinese Economy Post-Mao. A Compendium of Papers, submitted to the Joint Economic Committee Congress of the United States, Vol. 1, Policy and Performance, Washington 1978

Song Liwen
    Lun da li zengjia xiaofeipin shengchan, in: Hongqi, No. 6, 1981

Stepanek, James B.
    China's SEZ's, in: The China Business Review, March-April 1982

Tang Ren
    Zhongguo duiwai jingji maoyibu jiqi shuxia jigou, in: Jingji Daobao, 31.5.1982

Sun Zhen
    Qiye jiangli zhidu de jige wenti, in: Hongqi, No. 10, 1981

Wan Quwu
    Tiaozheng bili shixian shangpin gongxu pingheng, in: Jingji Yanjiu, No. 4, 1981

Wang Meihan
    Guanyu xiaofei jingjixue de jige lilun wenti, in: Jingji Yanjiu, No. 8, 1980

Wang Shanqing
    Buchang maoyi zhong zhide zhuyi de wenti, in: Shijie Jingji Daobao, 29.9.1982

Wang Shouchun; Li Kanghua
    Waimao tizhi de gaige, in: Hu Qiaomu (ed.): Zhongguo Baike Nianjian, Shanghai 1981

    Fazhan chukou shangpin shengchan jidi, in: Hu Qiaomu (ed.): Zhongguo Baike Nianjian, Shanghai 1981

Wang Yihe
    Woguo chukou maoyi pouxi - zou guangda chukou de xin luzi, in: Shehui Kexue, Shanghai, No. 6, 1981, reprinted in: Zhongguo Renmin Daxue Shubao Ziliao She (ed.): Maoyi Jingji, Peking, F 5, No. 2, 1982

Wang Yung-Ming
    China's Insurance and her Foreign Trade, in: China's Foreign Trade and its Management, Hongkong 1978

Weggel, Oskar
    Das Außenhandelsrecht der VR China, Baden-Baden 1976

Wiesegart, Kurt
   Oil from Chinese Deposits,   in: Intereconomics,   November-December 1980,

   Für Importunternehmen hängt der Korb höher, in: Handelsblatt, 8.2.1982

   Auch in der Außenwirtschaft soll der Wildwuchs weggeschnitten werden, in: Handelsblatt, 13.4.1982

Whu Zhenkun
   Guanyu jianchi jihua jingji wei zhu, shichang tiaojie wei fu de jige wenti, in: Wuzi Guanli, No. 5, 1982

Xu Dixin
   Woguo dangqian jingji tiaozheng wenti, in: Jingji Yanjiu, No. 6 1981

Xue Muqiao
   Zhongguo shehuizhuyi jingji wenti yanjiu, Beijing 1979

   Jingji guanli tizhi gaige wenti, in: Hongqi, No. 8, 1979

   Tantan shengchan ziliao liutong wenti, in: Wuzi Guanli, No. 1, 1980

Yamada, Yasuhiro
   China's Foreign Financial Position, in: JETRO China Newsletter, No. 35, 1982

Yan Cuiyou
   Tigao guding zichan biaozhun bu shi guangda qiye quanxian de zhenque zuofa, in: Jihua Jingji, No. 6, 1957

Yang Bo
   Jilei he xiaofei guanxi de tantao, in: Hongqi, No. 6, 1981

Yang Jianbai; Li Xuefeng
   The Relations between Agriculture, Light Industry and Heavy Industry in China, in: Social Sciences in China, Vol. 12, 1980

Yang Jisheng
   Lilun lantu shiyan tiaojian, in: Jingji Yanjiu, No. 4, 1982

You Lin
   Gaijin jingji tizhi de zhongyao zhidao wenjian, in: Honqi, No. 2, 1982

Yue Wei
   Guomin shouru jisuan fangfa lun, in: Jingji Yanjiu, No. 3, 1956

Zhang Peiji
   Stick to Open Policy and Expand Foreign Trade, in: Economic Reporter, No. 5, 1982

Zhan Wu; Liu Wenpu
San zhong quanhui kaichuang de woguo nongye fazhan de xin luzi,
Hongqi, No. 17, 1982

Zhan Guizhong
Ping "Jilei bizhong guding lun", in: Jihua Jingji, No. 8, 1958

Zhang Jingfu
Report on the Final State Accounts for 1978 and the Draft State
Budget for 1979, in: Main Documents of the Second Session of the
Fifth National People's Congress of the People' Republic of China,
Peking 1979

Zhao Xi'an
Lun yinhang zai jihua zhong de tiaojie zuoyong, in: Zhongguo Jinrong, No. 10, 1982

Zhou Ji
Woguo haiguan dui "haiguan jinchukou shuice" jingxing tiaozheng,
in: Guoji Maoyi Xiaoxi, No. 1, 18.1.1982, reprinted in: Zhongguo
Renmin Daxue Shubao Ziliao She (ed.): Maoyi Jingji, Peking, F 5,
No. 3, 1982

Zhou Shulian
Tiaozheng guomin jingji de jige lilun wenti, in: Jingji Yanjiu, No.
3, 1981

Zhou Zhuandian
Guanyu jiceng gongye qiye guanli zhidu de gaige wenti, in: Hongqi,
No. 7, 1981

Zhu Fulin; Xiang Huaicheng
Dui gaige caizheng tizhi de yixu kanfa, in: Jingji Guanli, No. 5,
1979

o.V.
China Needs More Foreign Investment, in: Economic Reporter, No. 5
1982

China's New Major Drive to Seek Foreign Investment, in: Economic
Reporter, No. 4, 1982

What's Happening in Chinese Joint Ventures, in: JETRO
China Newsletter, No. 36, 1982

Ba chukou shangpin jidi jianshe hao, in: Renmin Ribao, 19.6.1979

Fahui yanhai diqu youshi - jiaqiang duiwai jingji maoyi, in: Renmin
Ribao, 17.1.1982

Guangu woguo de duiwai jingji guanxi wenti, in: Hongqi, No. 8,
1982

PERIODICALS AND NEWSPAPERS

Beijing Rundschau
    Peking

Caizheng Yanjiu
    Peking

China Daily
    Peking

China Economic News
    Hongkong

China Trade Report
    Hongkong

Economic Reporter
    Hongkong

Far Eastern Economic Review
    Hongkong

Frankfurter Allgemeine Zeitung
    Blick durch die Wirtschaft,
    Frankfurt

Gongren Ribao
    Peking

Guangming Ribao
    Peking

Handelsblatt
    Düsseldorf

Hongqi
    Peking

Intereconomics
    Hamburg

Internationale Wirtschaft
    Wien

JETRO China Newsletter
    Tokyo

Jihua Jingji
    Peking

Jingji Daobao
    Hongkong

Jingji Guanli
    Peking

Jingji Yanjiu
    Peking

Nachrichten für Außenhandel
    Eschborn

Nengyuan
    Peking

Renmin Ribao
    Peking

Shijie Jingji Daobao
    Shanghai

Social Sciences in China
    Peking

Ta Kung Pao
    Hongkong

The China Business Review
    Washington

The Financial Times
    London

The Japan Economic Journal
    Tokyo

The Journal of Commerce
    New York

The Wall Street Journal
    New York

Wuzi Guanli
    Peking

Xinhua News Agency
    News Bulletin, XNA,
    Peking

Xinhua Yuebao
    Peking

Zhongguo Jinrong
    Peking

OTHERS

China: Socialist Economic Development, ed. by the World Bank, Washington 1981.

Communiqué of the State Statistical Bureau of the People's Republic of China on Fulfilment of China's Economic Plan (1978-1981, Peking)

Dokumente der 1. Tagung des V. Nationalen Volkskongresses der Volksrepublik China, Peking

Main Documents of the Second Session of the Fifth National People's Congress of the People's Republic of China, Peking

State Statistical Bureau: Ten Great Years, Peking 1960

Weltentwicklungsbericht 1980, ed. by the World Bank, Washington 1980

Zhonguo Baike Nianjian (ed. Hu Qiaomu), Shanghai 1981

Zhongguo Jingji Nianjian, (ed. Xue Muqiao), Peking 1981